# CHRISTIAN ORIGINS
## IN
## SOCIOLOGICAL
## PERSPECTIVE

£4 -
gen

7/40

# CHRISTIAN ORIGINS
# IN
# SOCIOLOGICAL
# PERSPECTIVE

Howard C. Kee

SCM PRESS LTD

334 01933 8

First published in Britain 1980
by SCM Press Ltd
58 Bloomsbury Street London WC1

Typeset in the United States of America
and printed in Great Britain by
Richard Clay Ltd (The Chaucer Press)
Bungay, Suffolk

# CONTENTS

# PREFACE

Along with many colleagues in the field of Christian origins, in recent years I have been drawn increasingly— and, I think, fruitfully—to various aspects of sociological studies as a potential tool for furthering my historical and interpretative work. Other trends in biblical studies in recent years have seemed to me to be pursued as ways of avoiding confrontation with the meaning of the texts, or at least of transmuting the apparent meaning into categories that are more respectable intellectually than the literal content of the New Testament seems to permit. What is the modern interpreter to do, for example, with miracles, visions, celestial ascents and descents, or conflicts with demons? Even in a gullible era such as ours, which seems fascinated by orthodoxy and/or the occult, many academics interested in primitive Christian literature apparently prefer to approach it by way of the metaphorical, the parabolic, the symbolic, or the "deep structures" in the universal human mind, rather than by the historical in its social and cultural dimensions. To borrow phrases from the late Henry J. Cadbury, the alternatives are not limited to modernizing Jesus or archaizing ourselves. What sociological methods seem to offer, and indeed, to demand, is the adaptation of analytical models from the social sciences as aids to (1) historical reconstruction—in as complete a manner as the data permit—of the development of early Christianity; and (2) interpreting the surviving evidence of the movement in a manner that is attuned to and sympathetic with the thought worlds of those who produced this material. "Sympathetic" implies an intellectual stance, a scholarly strategy for the historian-interpreter; it may or may not include a faith commitment to the claims of the evidence under scrutiny.

In the course of my recent work I have felt the need to sort out as systematically as possible what methods deriving from the social sciences may be of service for these kindred historical and interpretative tasks. Rather than merely identifying these methods and setting them down as intellectual abstractions, it seems more honest and potentially more useful to explore in a provisional way what might be the historiographical results of employing these methods. Included are not only methods that have traditionally been regarded as sociological but also those that treat of broader contextual, conceptual, and functional factors: anthropology, sociology of knowledge, sociology of literature. The opening chapter outlines the ways in which these approaches are utilized and, in addition, describes in broad strokes how earlier historians of primitive Christianity have correlated their historiography with nonhistorical factors, including philosophy, apologetics, didactics, and even sycophancy. Without denying that the current surge of interest in the sociological setting of early Christianity is a manifestation of the spirit of this age, I hope that this historical strategy will be of service in placing the ancient texts and documents in a context more nearly appropriate to them. What is written here is an essay in the root sense: an attempt, a trial run. It makes no claim to offer a finished product or to set forth assured results. But it is presented as a requisite step looking forward to the larger task of constructing a comprehensive picture of the social dynamics by which Christianity emerged and grew on the stage of history.

Material included here reflects my debts to and disagreements with colleagues—both those who work along similar lines and those whose ground rules differ from mine. I have built on my earlier publications and have benefited from seminars conducted in Boston, and from Waterville, Maine, to Denver, Colorado, as well as from discussions following guest lectures at Brown, Michigan State, Willamette, and Colgate universities. Some of the material has been prepared in a different form for the Lowell Lectures, offered at Boston University in October 1979, an honor for which I am indebted to my colleagues at Boston. Several friends have read the manuscript in various rescensions: Susan Purdy (Columbia University-Union Theological Seminary); Peter Berger (Boston College); Elaine Pagels (Barnard); Abraham Malherbe (Yale). I have learned from them all, but take final responsibility for what is here written.

The book is dedicated to the memory of my parents, who surrounded all their children with love, stimulation, encouragement, and humor.

H.C.K.

*Boston University*
*July 1979*

# 1

# INTRODUCTION

A quarter of a century ago, Henry J. Cadbury observed on the subject "Current Issues in New Testament Study": "More important than the immediate problems of origin, even those of exact date and authorship, are those of culture or *Weltanschauung*. To put it bluntly, I find myself much more intrigued with curiosity about how the New Testament writers got that way than with knowing who they were." He went on to characterize the problems that he thought should be addressed as "psychological rather than literary," adding: "It is regrettable that so little has been done and is being done to match the study of expression with a study of mind and experience."[1] The passing of twenty-five years in biblical studies has done more to draw attention to the issues raised by Cadbury than to resolve them.

As was true throughout Prof. Cadbury's long and distinguished career, he was ahead of his time in his plea for a shift of focus in research on Christian origins from literary to social questions. His own work on the cultural background of Luke-Acts has proved to be an enduring contribution to the field of early Christian history.[2] Yet in another sense, what Cadbury was calling for has been a perennial concern of thoughtful persons in the church almost from the beginning of the Christian movement, although each has understandably undertaken the task of historical investigation of Christian origins along lines shaped by the cultural setting and perceived needs of his or her own epoch. It may be useful, before outlining our own proposals for strategy and resources in the twin tasks of historical reconstruction and New Testament interpretation, to sketch briefly some of the representative ways in which historical work has been undertaken in the past, and why. In each case one of the controlling factors or organizing principles has been an aim or commitment extrinsic to the historical material itself.

## I

The reports of Papias about the origins of the Gospels, preserved in fragmentary form in Eusebius' *Ecclesiastical History*,[3] have two aims: to link the gospel tradition with Jesus and to attribute the authorship of each Gospel to an apostle or his aide. That is in keeping with what we might expect to be the historical interests of a church striving for unity on structural and doctrinal grounds—and hence stressing apostolicity—in the second century. Eusebius (ca. 263–ca. 340) obviously undertook his own historical work with Constantine's support and with the goal of lending respectability to the religion that the emperor had grasped as an instrument to stabilize his fragmented realm. As court historian-theologian, Eusebius tried simultaneously to flatter the emperor, lend divine sanction to his reign, and invite all Roman subjects to come aboard the imperial ark:

Our emperor, emulous of [Christ's] divine example [i.e., of the universal offer of salvation], having purged his earthly

dominion from every stain of impious error, invites each
holy and pious worshiper within his imperial mansions, ear-
nestly desiring to save with all its crew that mighty vessel
of which he is the appointed pilot.[4]

The lasting value of Eusebius' work lies not in the apologetic intent of the historical reconstruction he undertook
but in the archivist approach he used, whereby he preserved fragments from earlier Christian documents that
would otherwise have been lost to posterity—of which
Papias' *Expositions of the Dominical Logia,* alluded to
above, is an important case in point. Jerome (320–420), in
writing his *Concerning Famous Men,* drew heavily on
Eusebius for his information, but had his own distinctive
aim: to show by vivid example the appeal and value of the
intellectual life for Christians, and especially of ascetic and
monastic life-styles. And of course, he was himself a prime
exhibit of these ideals, at a time when the preservation of
Christian learning was centered primarily in monasteries.

Serious efforts at historical reconstruction of early Christianity through critical analysis of the sources did not
begin until the early nineteenth century. Rightly regarded as the prime mover in this undertaking is Ferdi-
nand Christian Baur (1792–1860). Like H. J. Cadbury a
century later, Baur was not so much interested in the
identity of the early Christian writers as in the factors that
shaped their understanding. Baur's early (1831) study of
the party strife in the Corinthian church[5] led him to see
that rather than an original unity within the Christian
movement there was conflict and sharp difference of opinion from as far back as the historian can trace. The two
main groups, Baur concluded, were the Pauline law-free
party and the Petrine Judaizing party. Later, these were
blended to constitute catholic Christianity of the late second century. In his later career Baur's view of early Chris-

tian history was increasingly influenced by the philosophical theory of G. W. F. Hegel (1770–1831), according to
which reality moves in a triadic pattern from thesis and
antithesis to synthesis.[6] Thus Acts "is the apologetic attempt of a Paulinist to facilitate and bring about the *rap-
prochement* and union of the two opposing parties."[7] Its
historical value, therefore, must be understood on two
different levels: the information about the apostolic age
which it reports, and the conditions of the postapostolic
age during which it was written. Both have historical significance, but each must be critically analyzed and recon-
structed.

At the turn of the twentieth century, the dominant
figure in the history of Christian origins was Adolf von
Harnack (1851–1930). In a famous series of popular lectures, *The Essence of Christianity,*[8] Harnack, in addition
to tracing the historical development of the church, reduced essential Christianity to the Fatherhood of God and
the infinite worth of the human soul. This idealistic ab-
straction enabled him simultaneously to treat Jesus as a
Jew of his time and culture and to extract from that socially conditioned setting the timeless essence of universal
religion. Harnack further concluded that neither Paul nor
Jesus was influenced by the Greek world, but that a radical
break occurred between the New Testament writers and
subsequent Christianity in that the latter was informed by
the Hellenic spirit. Thus Harnack could have it both ways:
he was free to investigate the post-New Testament development of Christianity without having to demonstrate historical links with Jesus and the apostles; but he knew apart
from his critical investigations what were the essential
elements of Jesus' message of the kingdom:

The kingdom . . . is something supernatural, a gift from
above, not a product of ordinary life. Secondly, it is a purely
religious blessing, the inner link with the living God;
thirdly, it is the most important experience [anyone] can
have, that on which everything depends, it permeates and
dominates [one's] whole existence, because sin is forgiven
and misery banished.[9]

By the middle of the twentieth century Rudolf Bultmann had come to dominate the field of New Testament
study through his own combination of tactics: (1) thor-
oughgoing critical analysis of the sources, and (2) the erec-
tion of a safe theological sanctuary. As Harnack had done
before him, Bultmann used a prevailing philosophical
mode as his standard for determining timeless meaning
and universal truth in the early Christian documents. In
Harnack's case, it was liberal idealism, but for Bultmann
it was existentialism, deriving mainly from the thought of
Martin Heidegger. The essence of the message and meaning of Jesus is his call to decision: by the obedient response
of faith, one dies to the "world" of culture-conditioned
values and is granted a new life by divine grace.[10] Critical
assessment of the Synoptic Gospels enables one to see this
behind the subsequent modifications of that tradition
which they embody in their present state, Bultmann asserted; but the clearest expression of this ultimate truth is
to be seen in the writings of Paul and the Gospel of John
—properly expurgated to remove later sacramental and
theological accretions.[11] Bultmann's least impressive work
is his *Primitive Christianity in Its Contemporary Setting,*
which is fundamentally marred by his credulous acceptance of now-discredited historical constructs (such as the
Gnostic redeemer myth[12]) that are supposed to account
for certain Christological developments in the New Testament, and by his creating a gulf between the timeless

Christian message (represented by the Jesus behind the Gospels, by Paul, and by the edited John) and the rest of the New Testament.

Ironically, in Bultmann's epochal form-critical analysis of the Synoptics, both he and his colleague Martin Dibelius had appealed to the social setting *(Sitz-im-Leben)* of the tradition as the clue to understanding its function in primitive Christianity.[13] Yet neither gave adequate attention to what the setting might be. Dibelius spoke vaguely of functional settings: preaching, teaching, worship. Bultmann made a distinction between "Palestinian" and "Hellenistic" settings for traditions, as though Palestine and its Jewish inhabitants were not pervasively Hellenized by this time, just as Jews were in the dispersion.[14] In Britain important investigations of the historical background of the New Testament had been carried on from the turn of the century, especially on the Roman world and the journeys of Paul,[15] but the major aim was to demonstrate the historicity of the text.

In Germany, Adolf Deissmann made a strong case for the hypothesis that the social and linguistic background against which the New Testament writings were to be interpreted was that of the nonliterary documents—the then recently discovered and published papyri, including business documents and private letters rather than the highbrow literature of the classical world—if the unpretentious literary remains of early Christianity were to be properly understood.[16] While Deissmann's inferences are in large measure valid, they have had to be modified by increasing evidence that nearly all the New Testament writers were strongly influenced by the translation-Greek style of the Septuagint, which almost from the outset became the Bible of the early church. Also qualifying Deissmann's literary judgments is the growing consensus that both the Jewish rabbis of the turn of the era and the early Christians were consciously or unconsciously imitating the practices and literary strategies of philosophical schools of Greco-Roman culture.[17]

In America between the two World Wars, the University of Chicago was the center for studies of the social evolution of early Christianity, led chiefly by Shirley Jackson Case.[18] As Robert W. Funk has pointed out, Case's major plea was that Christian origins be studied as social process rather than as literary or institutional history.[19] His own interests moved away from biblical studies, however, and the dominant intellectual discipline of the Divinity School at Chicago became philosophy of religion;[20] with regard to New Testament studies, Chicago became and remained for decades a center primarily for textual criticism.

Stimulated by the moral and political crises of the 1960's, widespread manifestations of search for social identity were evident on both sides of the Atlantic, in academia as well as among the general public. Among scholars in both sociological and historical fields, studies began to appear on millenarian movements.[21] The works of Max Weber on charismatic leaders and the dynamics of incipient or radically reformist religious movements were republished. By the mid-1970's, biblical scholars began to turn to the task announced by Case—and called for by Cadbury—of examining the social process by which the Christian movement originated, and to do so by employing methods derived from the social sciences.

Pointing the way for this approach to the historical study of early Christianity was the work of Peter Brown and E. R. Dodds on the social dimensions of the patristic period, with the attendant impact on individual piety and social identity.[22] In Germany, Gerd Theissen has under-

taken sociological analyses of Palestinian Christianity and
of the Pauline churches,[23] with impressive results. In
America, Abraham Malherbe traces and evaluates the
growing use of sociological method in biblical studies,
while seeking to show that Christianity was primarily an
urban phenomenon and that it appealed to a more highly
educated and culturally sophisticated stratum of society
than Deissmann or Marxist interpreters of early Christianity have recognized.[24] Representative of this development is the collection of essays by John Gager of Princeton
University, published under the title *Kingdom and Community.*[25] Here Gager draws on insights and methods
from Peter Berger and Thomas Luckmann (in the field of
sociology of knowledge), from Max Weber (in the analysis
of charismatic movements), and from K. O. L. Burridge
and others in relation to millenarian movements. The results are an illuminating and suggestive historical reconstruction of the broad outlines of the development of
Christianity from a millenarian sect, through a period of
incipient structure and discipline to the establishment of
the church in the Constantinian era. His method is "to
examine specific problems [in the rise of Christianity] in
terms of theoretical models from recent work in the social
sciences." Although his insistence on the importance of
social-scientific methods for historical study and his mastery of them are admirable, he concentrates his attention
on strictly social problems and tends to neglect or even to
avoid religious, theological, and hermeneutical issues,
which are themselves illuminated by the use of sociological methods. Our own approach seeks to employ those
methods for the dual tasks of (1) historical reconstruction
of Christian origins and (2) the interpretation of the literature which emerged from that movement. The aim of the
present work, therefore, is to make explicit a range of

methodological resources developed or developing in the social sciences that may provide fresh paradigms[26] for the analysis of early Christian literature with the aim of increasing understanding of the events reported as well as of the circumstances and life world of those by and for whom the reports were prepared.

So soon as one begins to speak of historical reconstruction, however, the factor of *interpretation of evidence* must rise to consciousness. In a widely used handbook of a generation ago, *History of New Testament Times,* R. H. Pfeiffer claimed he was presenting facts alone, on the principle that faith and facts do not mix.[27] He was unwittingly drawing on sources that themselves represented interpretations of evidence, and he had his own unacknowledged value system that was operative behind his historical reconstruction.

A more candid and fruitful approach is that proposed by Paul Ricoeur. In an essay appearing a year before Cadbury's note quoted at the opening of this chapter, Ricoeur discusses "Objectivity and Subjectivity in History."[28] Although Ricoeur is primarily concerned about the history of philosophy, his observations bear directly on the more general historical task. Defining history as "knowledge through traces" (a phrase borrowed from Marc Bloch), he declares that "the historian's apparent bondage of never being in the presence of his past object but only its trace by no means disqualifies history as a science."[29] To "grasp the past through its documentary traces is an *observation* in the strong sense of the word—for to observe never means the mere recording of a brute fact." The historian "goes to meet its meaning by establishing a working hypothesis. The trace is raised to the dignity of an historical document, and the past itself is raised to the dignity of an historical fact. By establishing the document, the historian establishes an historical fact." The process resembles that of any other science and is objective in that it is "a work of methodical activity."[30] The aim is not synthesis—to restore things just as they happened—but analysis. What is sometimes called explanation requires the historian to constitute a series of phenomena—economics, political, cultural—which comprise an ever more expansive complex. This work of recomposition can only come after analysis. It is the continuation of analysis and provides the ultimate justification of analysis. "Its near rationalism is of the same nature as that of modern physics, and in this respect there is no reason for history to have an inferiority complex." Like an Idea in the Kantian sense, the historian's goal of reconstruction is a never-attained limit.[31] At best the historian's subjectivity "represents the triumph of a good subjectivity over a bad one."[32] The historian must acknowledge this subjectivity and that he or she approaches the meaning of history with a preconception of what is to be looked for: "Whoever looks for nothing finds nothing." This is not a vicious circle so long as the reconstruction is seen as a history of consciousness rather than a narrow positivism.[33] The legitimate way to criticize such a historical undertaking is to write a "better history"; i.e., one that is both more comprehensive and more cogent.[34]

Ricoeur perceives the historian's work as animated by a will for encounter as much as a will for exploration. Only by calling up values held by those of an earlier era are we able to evoke human experience of a past that we cannot relive and to enter into the problematic of faiths of other times: "The suspended and neutralized adoption of the beliefs of past men is the sympathy proper to the historian." Here, Ricoeur is employing the special term "sympathy," advanced by Max Scheler, who has been designated the father of sociology-of-knowledge.[35] Scheler

distinguished sympathy from empathy, which is the supposed capacity to move by analogy from self-knowledge to
knowledge of others. He insisted that self and others must
be seen against the background of a common stream of life
experience: sympathy and love dispel the metaphysical
delusion of "relative solipsism."[36]

Similarly Dilthey came to recognize the limitations of
his earlier psychological approach to hermeneutics and to
assert that the individual must be understood in his
sociohistorical context: "Every word . . . , every gesture
. . . , every work of art and every historical deed is intelligible because the people who express themselves through
them and those who understand them have something in
common; the individual always thinks and acts in a common sphere, and only there does he understand."[37]

What is lacking among some historians of primitive
Christianity is the ability or the willingness to seek to enter
into the thought worlds of an earlier era—what Cadbury
called "mind and experience"—in which perennial
human experiences were differently perceived and therefore described in what might be called prescientific language and categories. In some quarters, however, the pen-
dulum has swung in the direction of credulity, of
willingness to accept the nonrational or the undemonstra-
ble in religion. The historian of early Christianity, however, cannot responsibly either abandon critical judgments or cling to an unquestioning faith in reason,
imposing modern conceptions on ancient culture. The al-
ternative to these extremes is not a simple balance ·be-
tween the two, but a disciplined effort to reconstruct with
"sympathy" the *Weltanschauung* (to use Cadbury's term)
of the early Christians in an attempt to understand more
fully and more precisely what they sought to communi-

cate to the readers of the documents we now call the New Testament.

## II

That the time is ripe for the joining of historical study and social-scientific method is evident from the side of the social scientists. In an essay entitled "Anthropology and History," written two decades ago but still articulating an accurate indictment, E. E. Evans-Pritchard deplores the antihistorical bias of many present-day anthropologists, whether those who abandon diachronic (tracing concepts and patterns through time, in terms of historical development) laws in favor of synchronic (describing concepts and patterns in relation to their own broad contemporary context) laws, or the functionalists who would account for cultural change by appeal to evolutionary laws. He sees close kinship between the work of anthropologists and that of social historians "who are primarily interested in social institutions, mass movements and great cultural changes, and who seek regularities, tendencies, types and typical sequences, and always within a restricted historical and cultural context."[38] There is only a technical, not a methodological difference between the work of the anthropologist and that of the social historian, according to Evans-Pritchard: the former studies people at first hand; the latter is dependent on documents. But both must rely on documents for comparative studies; both reason by analogy; both shift back and forth from abstractions to generalizations, or in Ricoeur's terms, from observation to meaning. "The anthropologist writes about the present in order to understand the past; the historian studies the past in order to understand the present." But both must move by analogy and contrast between past and present.[39]

From the field of social philosophy, and more particularly of sociology of knowledge, there is a consonant call for reconstructing the world view of a society in order to understand the specifics of its tradition and history. As we shall consider in detail in Chapter 2, what binds any society together is a vast set of common assumptions about human origin and destiny, about values, limits, responsibilities. Alfred Schutz and Thomas Luckmann have analyzed these phenomena and have given them a designation that serves as the title to their book: *Structures of the Life-World.* [40] Since the members of a society share a view of the world, they view their subjective experiences in typical patterns and stabilize their society by commitment to common values and institutions and symbols. [41] Knowledge about societies remote in time or space is provided through language, which enables the individual to transcend his or her own experience and thereby to interpret the past. [42] But when the historian undertakes a study of an earlier society it is not enough to note scattered historical analogies or contrasts; account must be taken of the shared view of reality in as complete and complex a version as the evidence allows if the details are to be grasped in a manner that is appropriate to the structure of the life world in which they emerged or were transmitted.

This sociological approach to knowledge has been appropriated and refined by contemporary sociologists of religion, particularly by Peter L. Berger. He acknowledges his debt to Luckmann in his illuminating, highly suggestive work *The Sacred Canopy: Elements of a Sociological Theory of Religion.* [43] The opening chapter of Berger's book touches only briefly on religion as such; its major concern is with sociology of knowledge: the way in which human beings construct a life world. This world is

comprised not only of the society in which the individual
finds meaning and identity, and not only of the culture
that the society transmits and in terms of which it defines
its own purposes, but also of the cosmic dimensions of
existence—what we would call the natural world, its origins, and the power that sustains it. When the norms and
structures of meaning that are discerned in subjective and
social experience are regarded as transcending human
limits and are accordingly projected on the universe, the
result is the construction of a sacred cosmos.[44] Both Luckmann and Berger recognize that of at least equal importance with what a society affirms about its life world is
what it takes for granted. Schutz calls this the "and-so-
forth" idealization,[45] by which he means those aspects of
common agreement within a society which are regarded
as self-evident, so that they do not need to be verbalized
but can be simply assumed and lumped together, as when
anyone abbreviates and concludes a statement with "and
so forth." A current cliché equivalent would be, "You
know what I mean." The fact is that the speaker does—
and in most cases, rightly—assume that his hearer not only
knows what he means but also shares his point of view.
This insight is of the greatest import in interpreting a
document, since the interpreter must be alert not only to
what is explicitly said, but also to what is implicitly assumed as common ground between writer and hearer.
The historian's task is to try to determine both what is
meant by what is said and what is assumed by what is left
unspoken. The student of early Christianity must be alert
to the network of implicit meanings present in the texts
of the New Testament writers.

The significance of the concept of "sacred cosmos" is
immediately apparent in the New Testament writings.
The Greek word from which our English term "cosmos"

derives is itself frequently used in the New Testament. More than 180 times the New Testament writers use the word *kosmos,* usually translated "world." It is to be differentiated from *gē* ("earth") and *aiōn* ("age" or "world"—"in this world or in the world to come"). *Kosmos* means the ordered structure of the creation and of human existence, individually and corporately, within that order, as well as the powers hostile to God and his purpose.

For at least two major reasons it would be a gross error if investigation either of the specific term *kosmos* or of the broader, all-encompassing conception as Berger uses it were limited to *theological* doctrines as such—even to the doctrine of creation. First, the New Testament writers did not share in every detail a common world view. There is a wide area of agreement among them, but on certain fundamental issues they are in significant disagreement. This involves not only theological differences, such as between Paul (Rom. 3:28) and James (James 2:14–26) on the subject of faith and works, but differences on such ontological questions as whether human beings are (Matt. 5:8) or are not (I Tim. 6:16) capable of seeing God. A physically realistic view of life in the age to come (Matt. 8:11, sitting at table with the patriarchs) stands in tension with the Platonic view of ultimate reality as spiritual, hinted at in the Pauline corpus (II Cor. 4:18) and explicit in later writings (Heb. 10:1; 11:16).

More is at stake in these differences than merely isolated conceptual details: what is involved is the larger question of the different stances toward Hellenistic culture assumed by various segments of the early Christian church. Some of the Hellenistic influence was mediated through Judaism; other aspects of it came from direct encounter between the Christian preachers and teachers on the one hand and the devotees of Hellenistic culture on the other. What is required in responsible historical inquiry, therefore, is the search for the various life worlds represented within the New Testament, rather than for a single common Christian life world. In Chapter 2 we shall raise questions about the sources and specifics of the various structures of the life world as they appear in the New Testament writings.

### III

Once the question is formulated about early Christian stances toward culture, however, the historian must be prepared to examine not only the conceptual aspects of that problem, but its social dimensions as well.

In speaking of sociological methods, two aspects of that field of inquiry and analysis must be kept in view: (1) the interior dimensions of social groups, by which groups form, merge, evolve, and by which leadership and group goals emerge and change; and (2) exterior aspects by which group identity develops in relation to the wider culture, both consciously (as in apologetics, propagation, and self-defense) and unconsciously (as in cultural conformity and various kinds of secularization). Without employing elaborate typologies for categorizing the stance of a religious movement toward the world (such as H. R. Niebuhr's theological types in *Christ and Culture*[46] or Bryan Wilson's anthropological classificatory system in *Magic and the Millennium*),[47] we shall consider the variety of stances toward contemporary culture represented by groups documented within the New Testament. By this means we can provide part of the response to Cadbury's question, How did they get that way? as well as the social-identity question, Who did they think they were?

A basic line of inquiry is the question of how the leadership launched the early Christian movement. The classic analysis of the widespread religious phenomenon of the leader as charismatic is that of Max Weber.[48] The charismatic leader well known in ancient Israel and in Judaism, is, of course, the prophet. He (or she) appears at the moment that a segment of society is faced with a crisis of loss of power or of meaning, or with a threat to the continuing validity of the hopes and aspirations of the wider society of which the alienated group is a part. The charisma of his personal gifts, his revelatory message, his promise of new meaning, rally followers around him.[49] Hans Mol has correctly noted that the charismatic leader is not so much a revolutionary as a reformer, a renewer of tradition. The prophet repristinates rather than innovates.[50] The intention of the prophet to appeal to the intention of the tradition, which has been perverted by the religious establishment, is a frequent feature of charismatic leadership, and one that has direct relevance for Christian origins. Exploration of these phenomena will occupy us in Chapter 3, where we must investigate not only the historical figure of Jesus, to the extent that it can be recovered, but also how and why he came to be portrayed in various ways by the later tradition. We must examine the leadership role of Paul, both in his relationships with the churches he founded and in his conflicts with other apostolic leaders. The depictions of the disciples and apostles in the Gospels and Acts must be analyzed in the light of what is known about leadership in emerging religious movements, ancient and modern.

The second factor has already been hinted at above: the process of formation of a group that regards itself as divinely delivered from the widespread perversion of the tradition and the corruption of the established leadership.

The sense of alienation from power and of rejection by its agents is matched by the conviction that the group has been granted a special insight into the purpose of God, which he is in the process of achieving in their behalf, or perhaps even through them. This belief in the divine self-disclosure becomes a central factor in the personal identification with the group. While analyzing the rise of early Christianity in these terms, it will be important to inquire as well about other religious movements in the Greco-Roman world that also claimed special revelation or access to divine mysteries. This will be our area of investigation in Chapter 4.

The third area to be explored in the light of insights and information provided by the methods of sociology of religion is to see how new religious movements develop their own patterns of ritual and myth, and other institutional religious forms. A major aspect of this line of inquiry is to seek to discover how tradition survives, how it is transformed, and what innovations occur under the impact of new needs or cultural forces. Mol has shown how the participation in ritual and the appropriation of a mythical tradition are essential features in a person's achieving and maintaining identity with a sacred group.[51] These dimensions of sociological inquiry are the focus of Chapter 5.

Finally, we shall consider the New Testament writings as such, seeking to discover the functions they were originally intended to serve. Here we shall draw upon insights and perspectives from the field of sociology of literature, as distinct from literary criticism. At least one current school of literary criticism insists that there is an "intentional fallacy" in criticizing a literary work by taking as the starting point the aim of the author.[52] The point is highly dubious, as E. D. Hirsch has shown, but even if it were to be regarded as valid, it would be appropriate primarily in terms of aesthetic evaluation of a work. Here our concern is with sociohistorical origins, not aesthetics. Our process moves forward by observing similarity and contrast, and by searching for clues as to intention within the writings themselves. We shall seek to discern not merely the aims of the writers of these documents but also the uses to which they were put in the early church. This line of inquiry can be carried out effectively only when careful attention is given to the world view that is maintained by the particular group in whose service the document was produced. Thus, it is in the study of each document as a whole that we shall discover the answers to such questions as: Why are there four Gospels, each of them written apparently for a different purpose? Why did Luke append to his Gospel the book of Acts? Why did certain writers employ a letter-like form for what seems to be essentially a theological treatise? Why do we have no Gospel in the New Testament that consists entirely of the sayings of Jesus, as we have in the apocryphal gospels and the recently discovered Nag Hammadi Gnostic library? Why does John's Gospel speak of God's love for the world (John 3:16) while yet differentiating the community so sharply from the world (John 17:9–16)? Did the conflicts between Paul and the other apostles arise out of purely theological differences or from differing conceptions of community?

Questions like these cannot be satisfactorily approached, much less adequately answered, on exclusively theological grounds. What we need to seek out is the nature of the community for and in which each was produced, and the function that these writings were intended to serve, as compared with the function that they came to serve in the later church. To find answers we need to turn to the categories and lines of inquiry suggested for us by sociological methods.

# 2

# CONSTRUCTING THE COSMOS

As we noted in Chapter 1, Alfred Schutz and Thomas Luckmann have drawn attention to the phenomenon that for all human beings the world of everyday life is "the province of reality in which man continuously participates in ways which are at once inevitable and patterned."[1] This world provides a realm of possibilities for action and limitations, some that can be surmounted and some that cannot. It consists of the self, other human beings, and a "coherent arrangement of well-circumscribed objects having determinate properties."[2] Anyone's attempt to explicate and understand the world is based on a stock of experiences, one's own and those transmitted by others—teachers, parents, etc.—which together constitute a stock of knowledge and provide the basis for understanding the present and making plans for the future.[3] The typical patterns of experience furnish the ground for establishing priorities and for actualizing life plans.[4] Included in this world are not only individual and group experiences but a view of the natural world, as well as a language and patterns of communication by which the world is interpreted and children or newcomers are incorporated into the group.[5] The transmission of knowledge becomes objectivated and socialized in signs and symbols, which are then passed on as myth or legend, and which take on the quality of the self-evident. The power and the validity of this socialized knowledge endure, or can endure, even when the original social relevance has been lost or forgotten. This "knowledge" is "of decisive importance for the development of a historical social reality as such."[6]

The handing on of objectivated knowledge is thus a major factor in the preservation of the identity of a society. But this convergence of factors also raises the possibility for inquiry as to the relevance of sociology of knowledge for historical reconstruction. If knowledge is to be transmitted by a society, there must be an ongoing social structure, which is to be preserved in its essential features. Even if radical changes should occur, the fact that the tradition is fixed in a written form enables it to be rediscovered, whether officially or by a minority element within the society. Also essential for the transmission process is the continuing relevance of the elements of knowledge.[7] Both continuity and change can be handled, however, even when radically atypical new knowledge leads to changes in the systems of signs or the constitution of new signs.[8] If the original element of knowledge "is fixed historically or mythologically," it occupies an important place in the hierarchy of knowledge and functions as an important feature of what is taken for granted in the society's tradition.[9] Schutz and Luckmann regard as "one of the most important tasks of empirical sociology of knowledge" the examination of such structural factors as the society's modes of communication and the contours of its world view—with special reference to the religious dimensions that serve to fix the tradition—since these factors "play a decisive role in the historical processes of the accumulation of knowledge."[10]

I

Long before the rise of Christianity these social processes of transmitting tradition and of giving it fixed historical and mythic form are evident in the religion of ancient Israel, viewed in terms of the nation's historical development. The twin foci around which the personal and social identity of the covenant people arose and is maintained are (1) the historic experience of deliverance from bondage in Egypt and (2) the Law, which gives stability and structure to the common life. Both the act of identification of the worshiper (Deut. 26:5ff.; Josh. 24) and the summons of the prophet to the wayward covenant people (Hos. 11) stress the divine action in history which is regarded as the originating event of the nation. When Elijah seeks to win Israel away from the worship of pagan gods and back to devotion to Yahweh, he begins the decisive act of sacrifice (I Kings 18:36) by addressing Israel's God as the sovereign deity of the patriarchs from the people's ancient past: "O LORD, God of Abraham, Isaac, and Israel." The prophets, charismatic figures that they are, are not portrayed as innovators but as those who recall Israel to her authentic historical and legal heritage.

There is in all this prophetic challenge no rational argument for the existence or the potency of Israel's God; there is only recollection of the common tradition. Even in as distinctive a book as Daniel, with its dreams and apocalyptic visions, it is Daniel's commitment to the tradition of his people—dietary laws, prayer, refusal to participate in pagan worship—that is the ground of his identity, the occasion for the threat under which he lives, and the guarantee of divine deliverance for him as part of the faithful remnant of God's people. In the Dead Sea community, the Teacher of Righteousness (or One Who Teaches

Rightly) by his very title claims to be the restorer of the
true interpretation of the divine will and the re-founder
of the true people of the covenant. Those claims are made
explicit both in such documents as the Scroll of the Rule
and in the commentaries, which bring out the true meaning of the Scriptures. This fidelity to the tradition is to be
rewarded by the eschatological act of divine deliverance
and vindication, when the faithful priesthood is to be established in the true worship of Israel's God in the
renewed Temple. There is no dissent with respect to any
of these strands from the mainstream of Israel about the
special relationship of Yahweh to his people, or about the
enduring validity of the law and the prophetic traditions,
or about the ultimate sanctity of the Jerusalem Temple.
The majority has betrayed or corrupted the tradition; the
minority encamped by the Dead Sea alone has remained
faithful to Israel's heritage. The validity of the community's scriptures, ritual, interpretative processes, and expectations are not supported by reasoned justification;
they are simply taken for granted.

When John the Baptist appears on the scene, the sanction for his role and his message are provided by the tradition: the garb of Elijah and the expectation of the final
Messenger (Mal. 3:1; 4:5). The community that he rallies
around himself is no novelty but the true "children of
Abraham" (Luke 3:8). The new "sign" offered by John was
baptism, although it may have had precedent in ceremonial washings among the Dead Sea community at Qumran. But the baptism with water became linked very early
with the baptism with spirit and fire (Joel 2:28–32) and
with the hope of eschatological deliverance, so that even
the seemingly alien practice of water baptism becomes
incorporated into the tradition of Israel, and does so by

providing the ground for group identity among members of the covenant people.

Both the sociological theory of the transmission of knowledge within a society and the historical analogies and precedents within the experience of Israel and of Judaism right down to the time of Jesus have obvious implications for historical study of early Christianity. Most important is the factor of continuity in the transmission process. In spite of fierce disagreements on details, the Pharisees, the Samaritans, the Essenes, and the various early Christian groups had much more in common than one might infer from the fervor of their differences. On the fundamental question of the nature of the covenant people, the answers involve shifts and even violent conflicts when one moves from the Pentateuch to Jeremiah or Second Isaiah, to Daniel and the Dead Sea community, to the Samaritans and the Sadducees, to John the Baptist and Jesus. But on the centrality of the people-of-God issue there is no disagreement, and on the abiding validity of the divine will as communicated through the law and the prophets there is a high degree of consensus. Similarly, in spite of wide differences in detail between the Passover ceremony, the eschatological meal at Qumran and the early Christian Eucharist, there is a common assumption among all three groups that covenant identity requires cultic covenant renewal.

## II

Obviously, to stress continuity alone would distort the picture of historical development within the biblical community. Without conscious repudiation of the past and its traditions, it was possible for Israel to adapt to new circumstances by accepting what we have referred to as new "signs" of the sacredness of the community and of the divine sanction for the processes at work in its history. Adaptation[11] is evident in relation to many themes from which we shall choose four for brief analysis.

First is the adaptation of the theme of creation. What is generally regarded as the older creation account in Genesis, Gen. 2:4b–3:24, is the more anthropomorphic. God infuses his breath into man's nostrils, shapes woman from Adam's rib, cools off by taking an evening stroll in the garden, and personally expels the disobedient pair from Eden. The other Genesis account (Gen. 1:1–2:4a) has long been observed to be more formal, limiting God's participation in creation to his creative Word. It stresses order in the creation and implies that cultic purity and Sabbath observance are human obligations rooted in the creation. In the book of Proverbs, however, the Word of God as creative instrument ("and God said") has been replaced by Wisdom, God's female consort and agent in creation. The basic notion that it was through Wisdom that God formed the creation is set forth in Prov. 3:19–20, but in Prov. 8 the concept is much more fully developed, with virtual personification of Wisdom. The cultural factor that led to this development is probably the influence of the Egyptian concept of the goddess Maat as the divine instrument of creation and of the maintenance of order within the creation.[12]

In the Hellenistic period the role earlier assigned to Maat was shifted to Isis, whose personal compassion and assistance to the suffering is celebrated both in mythology and in inscriptions that have been preserved at shrines, where the ailing claim to have been healed by her beneficence. The self-declarations attributed to Isis show remarkable resemblance in substance and rhetorical form to the proclamations of Wisdom in the Jewish tradition, espe-

cially in The Wisdom of Solomon, chs. 6 to 8.[13] Wisdom is
the instrument of creation, the champion of justice, the
mistress of destiny, the bestower of beauty and human
benefits.[14] When one takes into account Sirach and The
Wisdom of Solomon, in addition to Proverbs, these are
precisely the roles assigned to Wisdom in the developing
Jewish tradition. We shall see how this process of adaptation of the mediatorial, redemptive, and benefactress roles
of Isis surfaces in the Christian tradition as well. It is important to note that, although her role is seen as universal
in its effects, it is only those who contemplate Wisdom, and
are devoted to her, who share fully in her benefits. In the
communal sense, they are the recipients of her care and
compassion. That sense of group identity is evident in both
Judaism and in Isis piety of the Hellenistic period.

A second area in which "knowledge" undergoes social
adaptation in Israel is the problem of evil. An oblique
approach to the problem is offered in the older creation
story, where the snake and human prideful aspiration are
assigned responsibility for the advent of evil. The arro-
gance of power is likewise evident in fragments of tradition in Gen. 6, where refusal of creatures to accept their
assigned places in the order of creation elicits divine judgment.

It is almost certainly under Iranian influence, however,
that a real ethical dualism appears, according to which
God's chief adversary, Satan, sets out to thwart the divine
purpose, as in the contrast between the pre- and postexilic accounts of Yahweh's (cf. II Sam. 24:1) and Satan's (I
Chron. 21:1) responsibility for David's sinful pride in con-
ducting a census. The end product of this assignment of
responsibility for evil to Satan and his aides is hinted at in
the report of the conflict among the heavenly powers in
Dan. 10, but has come to full flower in the Qumran War

of the Children of Light and the Children of Darkness, wherein the celestial battle between angels and demons is coordinated with the earthly struggle of God's people for victory and vindication over their enemies. By the opening of our era, this way of accounting for evil and of anticipating its defeat is so well synthesized with the older biblical tradition and so widely accepted—taken for granted—that no justification for it need be or is offered. It is no surprise that one of the first of the cast of characters to appear in the Gospel narratives is the tempter (Matt.), or Satan (Q).

Closely related to this view of final cosmic conflict is the progressively adapted Jewish national expectation. The tension between Israel as a nation and Israel as God's people is evident at least as early as the traditions that underlie the books of Samuel and Kings. The surrender of the nationalist route to achievement of Israel's destiny is apparent in the exile and the conditions of the return, whereby the Jews are a client state of Persia, presided over by a pagan governor and an officially sanctioned religious factotum, who recalls his people to the law of Moses and reestablishes the Temple cultus. Even in the thrust for independent political existence under the Maccabees, the justification offered for liberation from the Seleucid rulers is that Jews will be free to worship God without pagan hindrance or dominance by pagan-appointed hierocrats. The fairly rapid degeneration of the Maccabean line into political collaboration (with the Seleucids and later with the Romans) and religious corruption brought about widespread disillusionment with this grand tactic of fulfilling Jewish destiny by political organs. The result was the rise of sects and conventicles that abandoned either nationalist hopes or common life in Jewish towns and cities or both. The Pharisees moved from politics to piety, as Jacob

Neusner has succinctly phrased it,[15] while the Essenes withdrew to the desert. Yet in withdrawing, both groups maintained a sense of the ineluctable *obligation to achieve and maintain the integrity of the covenant people.* Although the details of their expectations varied, they were united in their confidence that God would manifest himself through his chosen Agent to establish his rule in the world and to vindicate his faithful people. They differed chiefly over the stages and climax of the eschatological drama. The Essenes and other groups of similar bent remained confident that God had especially revealed to them the detailed steps he would employ in accomplishing his purpose for his own people.

This outlook derived certain features from Hellenistic culture, specifically from Hesiod's theory of the successive ages of human history, which Jewish apocalypticists adapted, as in the series of visions of the end in Dan. 7–12. But from the beginning of her covenantal existence, Israel's keen sense of divine purpose in history had led the people to expect that plan to move toward fulfillment in the future. Jews rejected the familiar notion found in the religious systems of her neighbors from premonarchic times down into the Greco-Roman period: namely, that God's primary concern was the maintenance of stability and order on astronomical and agricultural levels, so that the recurrent fertility of the earth and the precision of movements of stars and planets were sufficient signs of divine approbation and competence. The cyclical patterns of Baal and Anath, of Isis and Osiris, of Dionysus, were rejected as inappropriate for Israel. There were, of course, various annual feasts that in their origins and in more ancient interpretation were probably linked with the cycle of seedtime and harvest. But concurrently with Israel's post-Maccabean decline in political power there

came increasing attention to the future and the aspiration
to fulfilment in a new age.

The fourth adapted theme is that of order in the present
existence. After the law of Moses had been codified and
fixed toward the close of the exile, the immediate tasks
were (a) to interpret it as a way of demonstrating its ongoing relevance and (b) to teach it in order to guarantee its
survival as part of the living tradition of the covenant
people. In the Hellenistic period, however, a subtle but
pervasive influence bore in upon Judaism, which did not
pervert the devotion to law but added to it a new dimension. This influence came from Greek philosophy along
two different lines. On the one hand there was the impact
of Platonism, with its concept of eternal forms or patterns,
of which all earthly phenomena were imperfect, transient
copies. The law of Moses, viewed as the expression of the
divine will, was considered by some Jews to be of this
eternal order. Confirmation for that estimate of it was
found in the curious biblical passage in which Moses was
ordered to make everything according to the "pattern"
that was shown on the mountain (Ex. 25:40). Interpreters
oriented toward Platonic ontology, such as Philo of Alexandria and the author of the letter to the Hebrews (Heb.
8:5ff.), understood this to mean that Moses had been enabled to behold the eternal, heavenly archetypes of reality
when he was granted a vision of God on the mountain. By
identifying the law with divine wisdom, many concluded
that the true law was itself the eternal archetype for
human society.[16]

The other powerful influence on Judaism's conception
of order in this period was the linking of Mosaic law with
the Stoic conception of natural law. Once Law and Wisdom were equated, it was inevitable that the order maintained by Wisdom should be regarded as the function of

(natural) law. The universality of natural law and the special gift of law to Israel stand in tension with each other in some Jewish documents of the Hellenistic period, as Martin Hengel has shown.[17] But in other writings of this period the two laws, Mosaic and natural, are treated as interchangeable, as in the Testament of the Twelve Patriarchs, where homosexuality is denounced because it is contrary to the law of nature rather than because it violates an explicit Mosaic commandment.[18] In Testament of Naphtali 3, the Law is equated with the laws by which the stars move in their courses. This cultural adaptation is made easier by the linguistic fact that a Greek-speaking Jew, for whom Torah (instruction) has become *nomos* (law), could scarcely avoid making the conceptual connection. The way is open for broad and deep adaptations of the Jewish tradition under the impact of non-Jewish cultures when Jews are living under foreign domination, politically or culturally or both. The perennial problem becomes how to maintain Jewish identity in the midst of cultural pressures toward adaptation.

### III

Under these pressures, many Jews abandoned their commitment to distinct identity as the covenant people and became assimilated to Greco-Roman culture. This is evident superficially in the adoption of Greek names—a practice that we find among a number of the early Christians, including some of Jesus' disciples. Is what we see going on in this cultural conformity an instance of what sociologists have called secularization?[19] Berger defines this as "the process by which sectors of society and culture are removed from the domination of religious institutions and symbols."[20]

From literary sources as well as from inscriptions and archaeological excavations, there is abundant evidence of the extent to which Hellenistic modes of education and entertainment were adopted in Jewish Palestine down into the Roman period.[21] Gymnasia, stadia, theaters, baths, the use of the signs of the zodiac even in synagogue decoration, all attest to the pervasive influence of Hellenistic culture. Hengel has stressed, however, that the appeal of Hellenism, culturally, and the major involvement in Hellenistic economics were found among the wealthy Jerusalem aristocracy, with the result that the lower classes felt alienated from those in positions of economic and political power. Yet the aristocrats were scarcely numerous enough to have provided the crowds to fill the stadia and theaters for gladiatorial and dramatic spectacles offered by the rich to entertain and impress the masses. A major source of mass alienation in this period was the widespread disillusionment with the religious establishment. This was spurred by the fact that control of the priestly office was effectively in the hands of foreign powers, first the Seleucids and then the Romans, even though the aim of the Maccabean revolt in the early second century B.C. had been to achieve religious and political freedom. The grandiose Temple itself had been vastly enlarged in Hellenistic architectural style by Herod as a way of inflating his own international reputation and of ingratiating himself with his Jewish subjects. As can be inferred from the Gospels, a further evidence of secularization was the harsh reality that the ultimate authority in Palestine was the Roman emperor's agent, the provincial governor.

The effects of these shifts of life-style and of political, economic, and religious control from those who claimed to be agents of Yahweh to those who were unmistakably tools of secular power were deeply divisive within the Jewish community. The options open to Jews were several, including (1) going along with the Romans and their culture, (2) withdrawing completely from society to live a life of pure obedience in seclusion, (3) organizing a nationalistic revolt, or (4) redefining God's purpose for his covenant people. This last was the route taken both by the Pharisees and, in their own way, by the early Christians. Neither of these groups defined the role of God's people in political terms, though the historic ironies were that Jesus was condemned as a political pretender to the Jewish throne, the early Christians were executed as subversives, and the apolitical Pharisees came to be the Romans' choice as agents in establishing political stability among the Jews in Palestine. The irony continued, in that by the third century the Christians represented a political force which imperial powers had to reckon with. And by the fourth century Constantine came to regard the church as the single agency capable of furnishing the fragmented empire with a politically unifying center. He justified his decision on the ground of a vision and his consequent conversion, although historians have long regarded his adoption of Christianity as a shrewdly calculated move to gain political unity. But this raises a question about the definition of secularization. Is it a retreat of religious values and sanctions? Or does it involve the assigning of religious values to the secular world structures? When the Pharisees made an accommodation to Roman rule, did this Jewish group become "secularized"? Did the synthesis of church and empire Christianize the state by *increasing* "the domination of wider sectors of society and culture by religious institutions and symbols,"[22] or did this change represent the secularization of the church?

The factor of "secularization" has immediate implications for the reconstruction of early Christianity, since in the course of one century the Christian church underwent rapid change in the direction of institutionalizing what had begun as a spontaneous movement. Protestant scholars have assigned to that transformation the title of "Early Catholicism,"[23] often with the implication that the pressure toward unification of doctrine and ecclesiastical organization was a regrettable falling away from the pristine paradise of Pauline Christianity.[24] But is such a unitary picture of the growth of Christianity warranted by the evidence? Even if we eschew as unscientific the value judgment about the deplorable decline of the postapostolic church, how are we to assess the factors that contributed to the basic shift of the church from sect to fledgling institution?

Our task in what follows is not to evaluate the diversity and changes that are apparent in early Christianity but, as noted earlier, to describe them, and to do so not merely by applying theological analysis in the abstract but by employing the concepts and methods developed in the social sciences as a way of reconstructing the setting and dynamics that helped to shape early Christian life and thought.

Hans J. Mol thinks that the processes of change in the relationship between religion and culture of the sort sketched above are wrongly described as secularization when thus defined. Coming at the issue from the positive side, which he calls *sacralization,* Mol sees this to be a process with four dimensions: objectification, commitment, ritual, and myth. Stating Mol's argument in highly compressed form, what constitutes "the sacred" develops as a consequence of projecting an order "in a beyond where it is less vulnerable to contradictions, exceptions and contingencies" (=*objectification*). That order then provides the basis for an emotional *commitment,* which provides the ground of personal and social identity. Repetitive actions and articulations renew and make overt the commitment (= *ritual*). The story and symbolic account, which presents a verbalization of the origin, process, and destiny of that order, is embodied in *myth*. [25]

We shall have occasion to examine the details of this pattern of sacralization later on, but here it will suffice to focus on what happens in the process of historical development of a religious tradition. As we have just noted in the rapid survey of historical changes within Judaism in the Greco-Roman period, the movement was by no means exclusively or even predominantly in the direction of "secularization." Indeed, as we saw, the adoption by the official leadership of Hellenistic views and values spawned a whole series of movements, each of which claimed to be the conservator of the true tradition of the covenant people. Mol is fully aware that in the passage of time and the shift of historical circumstances, religions change, both conceptually and institutionally. He also acknowledges that there is a tendency for "specific religious institutions and orientations to become part of and like the world," for which process he suggests the term "institutional secularization."[26] For the process of change by which factors earlier controlled by religion gain independence, Mol prefers simply "differentiation," in line with the suggestion of Talcott Parsons.[27] The development of a religious tradition, therefore, takes place by what Mol calls "a basic dialectic between differentiation/integration" and "adaptation/identity."[28] Thus the religious community must cope with change and continuity simultaneously. It must adapt while remaining faithful to its heritage.

While the dialectical approach of Parsons, Mol, and others is to be preferred to the theory that religion changes primarily by secularization (= decline), it is essential for

the historian to keep in mind that what Berger understands by "secularization" and what Mol calls "institutional secularization" do in fact occur. In terms of Arnold
Toynbee's "challenge and response,"[29] the crisis created
in a religious tradition by a challenge from without is likely
to evoke a range of responses. The ongoing challenge to
Jewish identity by Hellenistic culture and political power
was variously reacted to by Jews, as we have noted, running the gamut from assimilation to revolution, mystical or
physical withdrawal from society, and the transformation
of Judaism into the first-century equivalent of the small-
group movements of the late twentieth century. The irony
is that the more completely acculturated the official Jewish leadership became in the Greco-Roman period, the
more zealous and determined large segments of the Jews
became to retain their identity as the covenant people by
adapting and transforming the previously prevailing
norms of covenant participation.

## IV

The most important outcome of the differentiation vs.
group identity dialectic in this period, for our purposes,
was the rise of Christianity. It would lead to gross historical
distortion to assume that there was a single life world that
was adopted by the earliest Christians from the outset of
the movement and throughout its early history. The historian cannot speak of *"the* Christian life world": like any
other human response, the reaction to Jesus and his message varied with the background and the convictions of
those persons who heard him or his gospel. The conflicts
that are documented in the New Testament, such as the
fierce disagreement between Paul and Peter (when prod-
ded by "certain persons from James," Gal. 2:12), are not

to be attributed to mere personality conflicts or strictly theological differences, but to basically divergent assumptions about human existence and about God and his purpose, both for the world and for his people. Paul presupposed the universality of that purpose; James stressed the particularity. No simple logic based on agreed-upon ground rules could resolve the issue, since different Christian leaders were operating on fundamentally disparate presuppositions.

As we noted earlier, later generations could attack Paul's teaching of justification by faith, not on the grounds of Jewish particularism, but because it was incompatible with the strongly Hellenized ethical approach which "James" saw as the essence of the new religion. Once more, what was operative was not a strictly theological tenet, but a world view that was seeking to synthesize what it regarded as the essence of Christianity and the best of Greco-Roman culture. That value judgment is demonstrated further by the somewhat pretentious vocabulary and literary style which the writer of the letter of James chose to employ.

More is involved than arbitrary choices in the shifting attitudes toward central theological concepts in the New Testament. Diversity and change are evident in connection with the idea of the resurrection of the just, for example. The view that resurrection means awakening the dead from their sleep in the dust of the earth is explicit in Dan. 12:2. That same notion of physical resuscitation is assumed in the *reductio ad absurdum* argument in Mark 12:18-23 and parallels, where life is expected to be resumed with all its former patterns of relationships; it would wreak havoc in the age to come if the law of levirate marriage had been observed, with the result that one woman had seven husbands in the next life. Jesus, of course, is represented by the gospel tradition as already beginning to distance himself from that literalist notion of revivification of corpses (Mark 12:24–27), although all he is reported as saying positively about the resurrection life is that those who have been raised are "like angels in heaven," which is not much help.

Paul, presumably more directly affected by various kinds of Hellenistic ontologies with a sharp differentiation of matter and spirit, draws a distinction between a "physical" and a "spiritual" body, though without disclosing anything about a spiritual body, other than that it is characterized by "glory," "power," and imperishability (I Cor. 15:35–50) and that it is not a body of "flesh and blood." Several times in his discussion of the resurrection in I Cor. 15, Paul uses the terms "immortality" and "the imperishable," both of which are less appropriate to the older idea of the bodily resurrection. In the pastoral letters (I Tim. 6:16; II Tim. 1:10), however, these terms are clearly linked with the notion of Jesus as an immortal being. On the other hand, the specific terms for resurrection, which are found with great frequency in Paul's letters, occur only twice in the pastorals: once in a liturgical formula (II Tim. 2:8) and once in a warning against false eschatological views (II Tim. 2:18). What has happened is that the post-Pauline tradition has shifted from a world view dominated by the eschatological dualism of Jewish apocalypticism ("this age and the age to come") to a characteristic life world informed by Hellenistic ontological dualism (the realm of the transitory and the realm of the immortal). The cultural shift from a Semitic—even a Hellenized Semitic—life world to a more completely Hellenistic one is already under way in these changes. And with it goes a fundamental change in the mode of future expectation: from a radical end of the age to a fulfillment in the realm

of the transcendent. The change is dramatically apparent
when one compares I Cor. 15:52, Paul's expectation of the
Parousia and fulfillment "in a moment, in the twinkling of
an eye," with I Tim. 1:17, "To the King of ages, immortal,
invisible," or with I Peter 1:4, which promises "an inheri-
tance which is imperishable, undefiled, and unfading, kept
in heaven for you."

The whole matter of *knowledge* of the divine purpose
is also understood in different ways in the early Christian
communities, some of those ways linked with Jewish antecedents and, especially in the second century, some of
them attuned to the philosophical traditions of Greece and
Rome. The common assumption of all the New Testament
writers is that God discloses his purpose through the law
and the prophets. Although in the Bible the role of wisdom
is not fully assimilated into this way of understanding revelation, through equating God's Word and Wisdom it was
possible to hold a largely consistent view of God's creation
of the world and of his self-disclosure to his people in the
world. While some of the Old Testament writings raise, at
least by implication, the problem of the rationality of faith
(Job; Ecclesiastes), there is no effort among the biblical
writers to develop rational arguments for the existence of
God and there is no dealing with the issue of theodicy
(though it is at least posed in Job). Knowledge of God
comes not by reason but by revelation. In certain Jewish
circles—most clearly in Philo of Alexandria—an effort was
made to correlate human wisdom as embodied in Plato
and the Stoics with the revealed truth of the law of Moses.
But apart from some traces in the letter to the Hebrews,
that approach to truth did not affect the earliest Christians
in a basic way.

For the earliest Gospel, Mark, and presumably for Jesus,
the news of God's purpose for his creation ("the mystery

of the kingdom of God," Mark 4:11) was available only to the faithful community; outsiders were divinely prevented from grasping its truth (Mark 4:12). This same view of truth as vouchsafed to the elect is found in the Q tradition (Matt. 13:16; Luke 10:23–24), where the blessedness of those who "see" and "hear" is contrasted with the prophets and others who were unable to penetrate the divine purpose. Paul likewise refers to the knowledge of the end of time as a "mystery" (I Cor. 15:51). He explicitly contrasts human wisdom, which he says God chose not to use in conveying truth, with the wisdom of God, which is His chosen vehicle (I Cor. 1:18–25).

Another esoteric concept of knowledge attested in both Judaism and early Christianity is that of mysticism. Gershom G. Scholem's classic studies of Jewish mysticism have shown the kinship between this view of God and the world and that of Paul.[30] Developing from a base in Jewish apocalypticism, the vision of God enthroned (Merkabah) becomes the spiritual goal of mystics in the late Hellenistic and early Roman period, just as it had been the experience that launched Isaiah on his prophetic mission (Isa. 6). The throne came to symbolize the divine rule, though it is portrayed in the literature (in so-called III Enoch, which in Jewish documents is known as Hekhaloth)[31] as lying beyond a succession of heavens and surrounded by an elaborate complex of principalities and powers, through whom the divine will is mediated and divine order maintained. Paul refers in passing to the heavenly vision (II Cor. 12:1–4) in which he "heard things that cannot be told, which man may not utter." Probably the transfiguration story of the Synoptic tradition (Mark 9:2–8 and parallels) points to the same kind of mystical transport, in which divine messages of vindication are communicated and the mystic is illuminated with heavenly radiance. The very fact that the knowledge thus conveyed is not to be disclosed ("he charged them to tell no one what they had seen," Mark 9:9) shows that we are dealing here with esoteric wisdom rather than with public, rationally appealing, and logically defensible claims.

In the Gospel of John a variant form of this mysticism appears. There the true covenant people is depicted as the flock of God, who alone possess the knowledge of Jesus and through him of God (John 1:14). Their participation in the Eucharist assures them of gaining eternal life (6:51, 53–54), though the "food" is immediately interpreted to mean the teaching of Jesus ("the words that I have spoken to you," 6:63). Perseverance as disciples of Jesus assures them of access to truth (8:32); indeed, Jesus *is* the truth and the sole way to God (14:6). Chapters 15–17 of John offer details of the mystical union of believers with each other and with Christ, culminating in the claim of John 17:25–26:

> O righteous Father, the world has not known thee, but I have known thee; and these know that thou hast sent me. I made known to them thy name, and I will make it known, that the love with which thou hast loved me may be in them, and I in them.

This perception of knowledge of God is literally a world removed from rational argument or from the attempt to develop a correlation between divine revelation and human reason.[32]

Much closer akin to what became in the second century the mainstream of Judaism—that is, the Rabbinic movement—is the world view implied in the Gospel of Matthew. It is devoid of mystical features, but it shares with the apocalypticists and the mystics of early Christianity the disdain of worldly wisdom or inductive argument. For it, truth is to be deduced from Scripture, not only now, but "till heaven and earth pass away" (Matt. 5:18). The assumptions under which Matthew and his readers are operating are apparent from the outset: that God's purpose, inaugurated through Abraham and Moses, culminates in Jesus (Matt. 1:1); that all the events connected with the coming of Jesus are in fulfillment of Scripture, and are thus the outworking of God's purpose; that Jesus is the ultimate interpreter of God's will, but that he interprets in a way which is the fulfillment of Scripture rather than the repudiation of the Mosaic tradition (5:17); that since Jesus' initial mission to Israel (10:5) was rejected by the nation's leadership (27:25), the covenant people is now redefined (21:43) and open to all nations (28:19). Life within the community is to be in accord with the new revelation from the mountain (5:1) and is to be regulated by judicial structures within the community itself (18:15–20). Even the term "Gentile" is no longer an ethnic designation, but a way of describing one who stands outside the true Israel (18:17).

Matthew's world view, while not wholly other than that of Paul or Mark in its assumption of the authority of Scripture and in its concern to redefine the covenant people, signifies by its strongly normative approach to ethics and by the rigidity of its community structure a significantly different kind of community. Its life world was one with which Paul would have had profound disagreement. The tone and rhetoric of its polemics imply that it represents a community which is in continuing and conscious conflict with the rabbinically oriented Jewish community. With that wing of Judaism, Matthew is in clear agreement (1) as to what the issues are, and (2) that the Jewish Scriptures are the enduring ground of authority in knowledge of the divine will. The differences come in incorporating into that life world the unique role of Jesus and in the redefinition of covenant participation.

Yet in Acts, the author portrays Paul as addressing the learned audience assembled in the Areopagus at Athens (Acts 17) in terms familiar to Hellenistic culture and employing the rhetoric that was a common part of popular Greek philosophy of the first and second centuries. Paul even quotes their poets in his attempt to make cultural contact with his hearers (Acts 17:28). The book of Acts as a whole uses the literary styles and narrative techniques of Hellenistic historians and popular fiction writers. The Christian apologists of the second century were to go even beyond Acts in seeking to utilize philosophical and ethical concepts of the pagan world in order to show the reasonableness of Christian faith.

What is at work here is far more than a shift of evangelistic techniques: the writers have clearly adopted a life world that is significantly different from that of those earlier Christians whose orientation was in apocalypticism or who were preoccupied with Jewish legal issues. So self-evident is it to the author of Acts that his apologetic strategy is the way to go about the propagation of the faith that he offers no justification for what he undertakes, apart from the highly personal observation in the prologue to Luke (1:3) that "it seemed good to me . . . to write an orderly account." Clearly, then, Luke can simply take this apologetic stance for granted: it is his "and-so-forth" idealization.

The dimensions of that emergent Christian life world— or those life worlds, since not all took the same paths— must be taken into account to fulfill the task of interpreting the early Christians' writings in terms of their context and their intentions. In stark contrast to the conviction that knowledge of the divine will is a mystery, as in Mark

4 and I Corinthians, is the well-known view of Clement of
Alexandria that the river of truth is one: thus the reason
the Greek philosophers have a grasp of the truth is that
they derived it from the law of Moses. Clement's role as
head of the Christian catechetical school in Alexandria,
and his structuring of his major writings—which move
from his *Exhortation to the Heathen,* through his *Instruc-
tor of the Young (Paidagogos),* to his more abstruse
*Stromata*—shows how "secularized" Christianity had become by the early third century.[33] Or should we say, how
sacralized Roman culture was becoming by that date?
From either sociological perspective, what occurred was
that a life world had developed on Christian soil which was
profoundly different from the life worlds of the apocalyptic and legal-authoritarian Jewish matrices out of which
the earlier Christian world views arose.

Thus far we have concentrated largely on the sociology-
of-knowledge distinctions that are implicit in the various
life worlds that have been briefly examined before and
after the rise of Christianity. But an essential feature of the
emergence of the new faith was the appearance of its
leadership, which both challenged the existing covenant
community and began to rally new forms of the people of
God. It is to the consideration of the leadership roles and
the inner dynamics of the Christian groups as perceived
in terms of sociological theory that we now direct our
attention.

# 3

# LEADERSHIP AND AUTHORITY

I

As Max Weber's classic study has shown, the emergence of charismatic leadership typically occurs in circumstances where there is a crisis of moral and political leadership, where the traditional framework of meaning and purpose is no longer secure, and where a segment of the populace feels itself deprived of access to power and of a sense of personal or social destiny. In such a setting, the charismatic leader articulates the concerns of the group that rallies around him, provides the adherents with a sense of direction, and does so either by defining the ancient tradition and aspiration in new ways or simply by calling for a radical break with the past.[1] K. O. L. Burridge's studies of millenarian groups that have arisen in modern times show that a precondition of their appearance is that the political system in power is relatively permissive, with the consequence that competing political claims surface.[2] The leader's proposed solutions for immediate problems raise the expectation and confidence on the part of his followers that he can provide ultimate solutions as well.[3]

What kind of person responds to charismatic leadership? We shall be investigating that phenomenon some-what more fully in the next chapter, but a few observations bearing on the interrelation between the leader and his people may be relevant here. Talcott Parsons has noted that the rise of such a movement under charismatic leadership leads to what he calls the intellectualism of a relatively nonprivileged group, which remains outside the main prestige structure of society.[4] The group that rallies to the charismatic leader is alienated, or what Mol calls "marginal"—a term he has borrowed from the field of race relations.[5] The marginal groups "stand on the boundary of larger groups or societies, neither completely belonging nor suffering outright rejection." Marginality, he observes, may be regarded as a liability for the creation of a stable society or for the establishment of a religion, but it can function "as an asset for, and even as the source of innovation, rationality, objectivity, efficiency, and individualism."[6] There is a dialectical relationship between the leader and the group, but the creativity and the renewal of the tradition originates with the leader.

Of the charismatic types depicted by Weber, the most appropriate one for our purposes is the ethical prophet. Weber portrays him as persuaded that he is the agent of the transcendent God, and that the precepts which he teaches are the expression of the divine will. The potency of his charismatic endowment is evident in the special gifts he possesses (such as healing or predictive capacities) and in the effectiveness of his preaching. Although the exercise of his gifts tends to confirm his authority, it is the persuasive power of the revelation which he claims has been granted him that is the ultimate ground of his effectiveness.[7]

Leaders of this type arise in times of psychic, physical, economic, ethical, religious, or political distress. They were not previously officeholders, nor are they gainfully employed in a regular occupation. Rather, they are seen to possess specific gifts of the body and the spirit, and "these gifts have been believed to be supernatural, not accessible to everybody." Their assumption of their role knows nothing of an ordered procedure of appointment or dismissal; there is no regulated career, advancement, salary, or expert training, just as there is no agency of control or appeal, no delineation of jurisdiction or territory. And the enterprise gives rise directly to no permanent institution. "The holder of charisma seizes the task that is adequate for him and demands obedience and a following by virtue of his mission."[8]

The paradox of charismatic leadership is that, while appealing to persons who are alienated from the power centers of a society, its program is not represented as revolutionary but as a combination of (1) protest against a corrupt or hypocritical regime and (2) of promoting a return to the essence of the tradition.[9] This is clearly evident in the role of the prophets of ancient Israel, who were not opposed to the cult or to the historical tradition, but who wanted to purge it of distortion and corruption. They see themselves and are seen by their adherents not as breaking with the past but as recovering a lost or perverted heritage. Accordingly, the role of the charismatic leader is "reintegrating rather than revolutionizing society."[10]

Our procedure in exploring the relevance of the charismatic leader for the historical reconstruction of early Christianity will be to look at some historical models from the Greco-Roman period in order to discern both typical and distinctive features of the leadership roles in early Christianity.

## II

From both literary and historical sources, it is possible to trace certain patterns of charismatic leadership within both Jewish and pagan social contexts in our period. Josephus describes in his *Jewish War* how, given the political instability that plagued Palestine after the death of Herod (4 B.C.), there arose a series of insurrectionists, culminating in the initially successful actions of revolutionaries in A.D. 66 and the years immediately following. In that year the seriousness of the nationalist threat to Rome was signaled and symbolized by the insurgents' capture of the seemingly impregnable fortress of Masada,[11] with the consequent breaking off of sacrifices in the Jerusalem Temple in behalf of the Roman ruler.

Prior to this climactic event, there were not only other revolutionary figures and royal pretenders[12] but persons committing seemingly senseless acts of terrorism. Josephus gives no hint of their aims, though he distinguishes them from the "brigands" (which is his code word for insurrectionists, a term which his pro-Roman bias led him to avoid in describing his fellow countrymen). The "daggermen" he depicts mingling with the crowds, performing random murders; yet neither their aims nor their identity became clear, at least in Josephus' account.[13] But the consequence was a pervasive anxiety:

> The panic created was more alarming than the calamity itself; everyone, as on the battlefield, hourly expecting death. Men kept watch at a distance on their enemies and would not trust even their friends when they approached.[14]

Following immediately on the account of this reign of terror, Josephus describes what was chronologically and logically linked with the period of profound anxiety: the emergence of charismatic leaders. Unnamed prophets are

said to have rallied groups of followers on the basis of a
claim to having been granted a divine revelation about the
deliverance of Israel from her foreign masters, the Romans. The groups were led out into the desert, perhaps in
conscious reenactment of Israel's initial conquest of the
land of Canaan in the days of Joshua. The largest such
following was rallied by an "Egyptian" (whether Jewish or
Gentile is not indicated) who rounded up a force of 30,000
and attempted a grand entrance into Jerusalem by way of
the Mount of Olives as prelude to his takeover of the city
in fulfillment of his prophetic role.[15] Instead of the expected miraculous deliverance, the fanatics were met and
decimated by Roman troops.

Any period of political crisis is an appropriate time for
the rise of such a prophet. The sharper the issue, the
clearer is the focus of the prophetic message. In the late
biblical Jewish tradition, this is evident in Daniel, where
the continuing threats to Jewish identity in the form of
proscription of prayers and dietary laws have been over-
shadowed by the impending horror predicted in obscure
terms: "Upon the wing of abominations shall come one
who makes desolate" (Dan. 9:27), which is almost certainly
an allusion to the heathen sacrifices offered up in the
Jerusalem Temple by order of Antiochus IV Epiphanes
after his profanation of Jerusalem and his campaign for
self-deification. The list of his cruel and blasphemous acts
against the Jews and their sanctuary is offered in the interpretation of Daniel's first vision (Dan., ch. 7, especially v.
25). Martyrdom of the faithful is expected and accepted,
but final vindication—and in the near future—is surely
anticipated, as the direct transition from prediction of ultimate horror to final deliverance implied (e.g., Dan 7:21-
22). The present political and religious crisis is considered
by the esoteric group that is being addressed in Daniel as

a time of confident expectation, not an occasion for despair. Whether Daniel is a pseudonym for an actual leader in this period or the spokesman through whom the seer and dreamer (who is this community's medium of revelation) addresses his conventicle cannot be determined. But the words of assurance with which the book ends (Dan. 12:5–10) are intended not merely for the seer himself but for all the "wise" who "shall understand." Similar roles are assigned to "Enoch," "Moses," and other patriarchs in whose names other Jewish apocalypses were written. In each case, the revelation of the impending divine deliverance is vouchsafed only to the faithful elect minority, who have stood apart from the main body of Jews dominated by corrupt leaders.

Similarly, in Mark 13 and parallels, Jesus is portrayed as addressing the faithful remnant in the days preceding the final judgment and ultimate deliverance of God's people. The inner circle is addressed "privately" (Mark 13:3). Even the written form of the apocalyptic pronouncement has a special meaning for the readers who can "understand" (13:14). The imagery, the technical terminology ("desolating sacrilege" = "abomination that makes desolate"), and the title of the agent of deliverance, Son of Man, derive from Daniel. The elect are the only ones who can discern the meaning of the catastrophic events that are now taking place and that will culminate in unprecedented horror ("such tribulation as has not been from the beginning of the creation which God created until now," 13:19); they alone will share in the final redemption (13: 27). Their life world is in process of being confirmed; they await ultimate corroboration. Likewise Paul allows his readers to share in eschatological mysteries (I Cor. 15:51).

It was not in Judaism alone that there was precedent for revelatory notions about history and its ultimate meaning.

From the eighth century B.C. on, there are reports of oracles uttered by the Sibyl (later, *sibyls,* located at various
cultic centers throughout the ancient world). The term, of
unknown origin, was used of a female revelatory figure
who predicted the course of history, concentrating chiefly
on dire calamities yet to come. Like the oracle of Apollo
at Delphi, the Sibyl uttered her pronouncements in hex-
ameter. Her predictions were collected in various places;
copies of utterances from the famous Sibyl of Cumae, near
Naples, were preserved in Rome. Virgil describes the Cu-
mean Sibyl's cave in his *Aeneid,* and in the Fourth
Eclogue he quotes her prophecy of the epoch of blessing
and abundance that is about to dawn with the accession to
the throne of a new ruler, probably Caesar Augustus, portrayed in terms of Egyptian and Iranian mythology.[16]

The Jews of Alexandria took over not only the form of
the pagan Sibylline oracles, but even some of their content. By showing that the "prophecies" about earlier
events had already come true, they wanted to advance the
claim for their own predictions about God's purpose in
history as they understood it. Thus the oracles of the Sibyl
in Jewish hands became an instrument of propaganda to
demonstrate the credibility of the Jews' faith in the God
of Israel.[17] The social function of these oracles was quite
different from that of the apocalypses, which were private
instruction for the ingroup, encouraging them to accept
persecution or even martyrdom in the face of human and
demonic opposition. Although both the Sibylline oracles
and the Jewish apocalypses shared the feature of purporting to have been written at an earlier period (history as
future), the respective roles of the revealers differ. The
Sibylline oracles were attributed to shadowy figures whose
chief importance lay in the pronouncements produced by
them or in their names, but the apocalypses were pro-

duced by or transmitted through charismatic leaders to whom revelatory knowledge of the future had been granted. The Sibylline oracles, pagan and Jewish, testify to how large and culturally diverse was the audience in the Greco-Roman period that was ready and eager to receive eschatological disclosures.

## III

A second type of charismatic role that has been the subject of extensive research recently is that of the miracle worker.[18] Building on an undocumented assertion by Rudolf Bultmann that Mark, in recounting the miracles of Jesus, is portraying him after the model of the Hellenistic divine man,[19] several scholars have developed elaborate theories about Christian origins on the assumption that there was a clearly defined designation for a miracle worker ("divine man") and that the accounts of his exploits were reported in a fixed literary form ("aretalogy"). Neither assumption is supportable from the evidence. There is a widespread tradition in Greco-Roman literature about philosophers whose wisdom, integrity, compassion, and pattern of life in conformity to the laws of nature were such that they were regarded as divine men. This did not imply their deification, but rather that they were attuned to and obedient to the divine. There is also considerable evidence from literary sources and from ancient inscriptions that at the shrines of certain Hellenistic divinities, especially Isis, pronouncements were solemnly uttered or inscribed about the deeds of the divine benefactor/ benefactress in behalf of the lame, the blind, etc. The strengths or virtues *(aretai)* of the divinity were recorded for posterity in an aretalogy.[20] While it is true that in some cases miracles were reported as being performed by philosophers, the divine-man tradition is basically concerned with philosophers as wise men. The aretalogical tradition on the other hand, consists of praise for beneficent deities. The miracle-worker theme in Judaism seems to have been derived, however, not from either of these pagan Hellenistic models, but from the Old Testament tradition in which God's acts in history are confirmed by his granting miraculous powers to his spokesmen—Moses, Elijah, Elisha, Daniel. These miracle-working agents are called "men of God," not divine men (II Kings 1:9, 11; 4:9). Similarly, the miracles described in the Qumran documents are seen as signs of divine favor rather than as evidences of divinization of the leadership of the community.

In the Synoptic tradition, Jesus is pictured as a miracle worker whose exorcisms and healings are signs of the advent of the rule of God (Luke 11:20) and as evidence that his work is in fulfillment of prophecy (Luke 7:22). The links between Jesus' activity and that of the earlier men of God, (Moses, Elijah, and Elisha) is explicit (Luke 4:24–27; Matt. 16:14; Mark 9:4). In the Johannine tradition, on the other hand, where the divine origin of Jesus is asserted from the outset (John 1:1–3, 14), the signs are linked with Jesus' divine glory (John 2:11; 3:2; 20:30–31). In both form and content they come closer than do the Synoptic miracle stories to the Isis aretalogies. And the "I Am" pronouncements of John's Gospel closely resemble the self-proclamations of Isis, which in turn show kinship with the figure of Wisdom.[21]

Ancient and modern critics of miracle workers have leveled the charge that those who claim to perform miracles are either magicians or charlatans. Lucian of Samosata (second century A.D.) wrote a satirical account of one Alexander, whom he styles "the False Prophet." In it he describes how Alexander's miracles are carefully contrived to deceive "the fatheads" and thereby to enhance his own reputation. Celsus (mid-second century A.D.) takes the same general position with regard to Jesus' alleged miracles: that Jesus may have performed the acts attributed to him in the Gospels, but that he did so by means of tricks and stunts that deceived his observers. In Celsus' opinion, there was no difference between the Christian exorcists, who invoked the name of Jesus, and the pagan magicians, who appealed to their own sources of magical power.[22] Some modern historians treating of this aspect of the Gospel tradition similarly discern no sharp distinction to be made between miracle and magic, in and out of the Gospel tradition, and accordingly engage in their historical reconstruction of Jesus and his career on the assumption that he was a magician and that his activity should be analyzed under such rubrics as magic or shamanism.[23] Is such a distinction possible and historically useful? Do the analyses of magic and miracle offered by anthropologists and sociologists of knowledge enable us to discern those features of these phenomena which are distinctive to the early Christian tradition as well as those shared with other cultures?

Among modern anthropologists the classic differentiation between magic and religion is that of B. Malinowski, in *Magic, Science and Religion.*[24] He described magic as the human being's way of dealing with those "impasses where gaps in his knowledge and limitations of his early power of observation and reason betray him at a crucial moment." The person's "spontaneous outbursts" and "rudimentary modes of behavior" in these critical circumstances become standardized. These beliefs and ritual techniques "bridge over the dangerous gaps in every important pursuit," and become fixed as the defined procedures for dealing with recurrent crises or warding off evil threats. Magic thus "enables man to carry out with confidence his important tasks, to maintain his poise and his mental integrity in . . . the throes of . . . despair and anxiety."[25] Unlike magic, which remains from earliest times in the hands of specialists (i.e., wizards and witches), religion is "an affair of all, in which everyone takes an active and equivalent part." Through belief and ritual, religion "establishes, fixes, and enhances all valuable mental attitudes, such as reverence for tradition, harmony with environment, courage and confidence in the struggle with difficulties and at the prospect of death."[26] Magic is a mode of action to achieve a specific goal;[27] religion "establishes not only a social event in the life of the individual" but also creates a pattern of social behavior and corporate responsibility.[28]

Other anthropologists have defined the difference between magic and religion (or miracle) in more nearly functional terms. Marcel Mauss sees magic as operating by constraint and direct, automatic efficacy; religion achieves its objectives through differentiated, spiritual intermediaries.[29] Lucy Mair, while acknowledging that we are treating here of the ends of a continuum rather than tightly separate categories, offers the following distinction: magic is concerned with the manipulation of forces; religion is occupied with communication among beings. Both share the aim of seeking to attain ends that are unattainable by ordinary human means. The efficacy of religion turns on contacting and procuring the aid of the proper divine beings.[30] The performance of rites is confirmatory of the religious community and the mutual moral obligations that bind it together.[31]

In a direct criticism of Malinowski's theoretical distinctions, Judith Willer's essay on sociology of knowledge proposes sharply separated categories for magic, religion, and science. For her, magic is practical (devoid of a theoretical base) and empirical, simply claiming that this act will produce this result. Religion she regards as knowledge that combines concept to concept rationally, based on an abstractive linking of the concept with the observable. In religion, cause is not attributed on the basis of mere temporal sequence, but is a theological consequence based on a concept. "All conditions and events are effects of the same cause and must be explained with reference to rational concepts."[32] Making a plea for a reasoned synthesis of the empirical and the rational, she observes that a science constructed on purely empirical grounds would resemble magic, while a science based on rational grounds alone would resemble religion.

Although Willer's criticisms of Malinowski are in part justified, they are also overdrawn. Religion cannot be fittingly characterized as the rational combination of concept with concept or as operating on a rational cause-and-effect basis. What is valid about her distinction is her depiction of magic as eminently practical. More cogent and illuminating than Willer's observations are those of Mauss, with his stress on automatic efficacy in magic, and of Mair, with her representation of magic as preeminently the manipulation of forces. As a whole, the Greek magical papyri bear out these characterizations; they pay careful attention to the details of thaumaturgic process (the circumstances accompanying the magical rites—such as the time of day; the phase of the moon; the magical word[s]; the material on which the magical formula is written, e.g., bat wings); and they proceed in the expectation that the properly executed process will coerce the unseen powers to grant the demands of the petitioner. The demon is ordered to act in response to the recitation of the incantation or the performance of the ritual. John Ferguson observes that in magic, achieving the desired result depends on correct performance; in religion, "the result depends on the will of the personal god." But he also notes that in practice the two realms may mix.[33]

Does this mean that miracle and magic cannot be differentiated in the New Testament? If we adopt the distinction offered by Lucy Mair, we can say that most New Testament miracles are depicted as the outcome of communication with a Being, rather than as the inevitable outcome of the manipulation of forces. Miraculous results are achieved in the New Testament accounts, not by thaumaturgic technique alone, but in direct response to an appeal to God or to Jesus as God's agent. The world view implicit in these miracle stories is one in which God's aid is solicited in overcoming the powers of evil. There are, however, New Testament stories that include involuntary manifestations of divine power, such as the healing touch of Jesus' garment (Mark 5:25–34 and parallels), the beneficial effects of Peter's passing shadow (Acts 5:15), or Paul's deliverance from the effects of the viper (Acts 28:1–6). But the occasional story within the New Testament that seems more nearly akin to magic than to miracle does not invalidate the distinction, nor does it warrant ignoring the differences between the respective world views that lie behind magic and miracle. As G. van der Leeuw noted, a miracle's essence lies in its character as a sign of divine power, and therefore in its revelatory content.[34]

It would be easy for modern historians to regard interest in magic and miracle as a symptom of the decay of traditional religions or as a largely proletarian phenomenon. This would be a historical error, however. Peter Brown has observed that both sorcery and counter measures to combat it "occur in precisely those areas and classes which we know to have been the most effectively sheltered from brutal dislocation—the senatorial aristocracy, for instance, and the professors of the great Mediterranean cities." Misfortune in such circles was interpreted as resulting from magical plots by one's enemies. The learned first-century encyclopedist Pliny the Elder wrote, "There is no one who is not afraid of becoming the subject of lethal spells."[35] To discover traces of magic in early Christian documents would tell us little about the social niveau of the movement, although the mounting concern with magic in second- and third-century Christian writings is consonant with the historical picture of the growth of both the fear and the practice of magic in the upper levels of Roman society.

As the historian E. R. Dodds has noted, what separated those who believed in magic from those who did not was not social or economic status: "The ancient debate on miracles was in the main a conflict not between believers and rationalists but between two sorts of believers."[36] Intellectual sophisticates like Pliny the Elder, Plotinus, and Libanius believed themselves to have been subjected to magical attack, and Dodds points out that even the skeptic Celsus acknowledged that perhaps the Christians did perform miracles, but did so by means of magic or by being in league with an evil demon.[37]

By contrast, it was the powerless persons in the middle and lower classes who were open to religion, with its larger hopes of personal and social meaning.[38] Thus, modern assumptions that blend together magic and miracle or that attribute gullibility predominantly to the lower classes are historically irresponsible.

IV

A third type of charismatic leader that must be analyzed for our purposes is that of the itinerant charismatic teacher-philosopher. Martin Hengel noted that Jesus' call of his disciples to "follow" him does not fit well with what we know of rabbinic practices of that time, which would have focused on study. Jesus, Hengel suggested, is more like a Cynic itinerant preacher-teacher than a rabbi.[39] Agreeing with Hengel that the content of Jesus' preaching was the prophetic-eschatological announcement of the end of the age, Gerd Theissen went on to suggest in some detail the similarities—as well as important differences—between the Gospel picture of Jesus' ministry and the role of the wandering radicals in the Cynic tradition, who were free of home, family, and possessions. Even the description of the limitations as to equipment required of the disciples (Luke 9:3) demands comparison with that policy decreed for the Cynics. The Christian itinerants were allowed no knapsack, no staff, no bread, no money. Both Christians and Cynics were to live on whatever hospitality was provided them. The fact that the restrictions on the Christian itinerants were more severe than those placed on the Cynic preachers (who *were* allowed cloak, knapsack, and staff, and lived by begging), suggests that there was a conscious differentiation between the Christian charismatics and the Cynics, even though the basic methods of itinerancy and public preaching were so similar. The Cynics' basis for avoidance of family or financial obligations was freedom itself; the Christians' motivation was to be free of ties in this age in order to be ready and to prepare others for the age to come. In this light, the sayings of Jesus "express the harsh realities of a homeless, protectionless existence like the birds'."[40] This pattern of life is presupposed in the *Didachē,* and is that of Peregrinus, whose pilgrimage from Christian itinerancy to a Cynic type of vagabond monastic life-style, is described by Lucian of Samosata. Quoting Max Weber, Hengel recalls that in the case of this type of charismatic leadership, the master as well as his disciples must be free of daily work and family obligation, except within the group.[41]

From Greek and Roman sources we know that the preacher-teacher who denounced the present order, on philosophical or other grounds, was regarded as a threat to order and an enemy of the state. The models for these self-styled philosophers were Socrates, who had died on trumped-up charges of being a subverter of the young and a disturber of the peace in Athens, and Diogenes, who heaped scorn on conventions and made even Alexander the Great appear ridiculous in a famous exchange.[42] By the middle of the first century and on into the second century, these itinerant mendicant emulators of the Cynics were a familiar sight in large and small cities throughout the empire, from Syria to Rome itself. Ramsay Mac-Mullen, in his book significantly titled *Enemies of the Roman Order,* has depicted them as follows:

> Teachers themselves, those of the rougher sort, appeared in every part of the empire from Italy eastward, in one of the commonest of the literary clichés: identified by their long hair, beards, bare feet and grimy rags, their wallets, staffs, and knapsacks; by their supercilious bearing, paraded morals, scowling abuse and rodomontade against all men and classes; shameless they seemed, and half-educated, vulgar, jesting; beggars for money, beggars for attention, parasites on patrons, or petitioners at the door, clustered at temples or street corners, in cities and army camps; loudmouthed shouters of moral saws driven to a life of sham by poverty.[43]

Despised by those who considered themselves true intellectuals as lacking in logic or real learning, and by the rulers as threats to the stability of the state, these itinerants spoke to the frustrations and anxieties of the masses. One Cynic philosopher so annoyed a succession of emperors that they tried by bribe, threat, and exile to silence him. Even a wealthy philosopher of quite different persuasion like Seneca, who served as court adviser to Nero, came under suspicion of the emperor, and finally was forced to commit suicide.

So long as Stoic philosophy limited itself to lofty theories and to hypothetical intellectual problems, such as Seneca's earlier treatise on whether the three hundred Spartans left at Thermopylae should have fled, it was welcome in the drawing rooms and aristocratic gathering places of the empire. The Cynic style, on the other hand, with its mingled words of comfort, social criticism, and hope, was widely received by the crowds in the marketplaces throughout the Mediterranean world. The potential of these strolling preachers for fomenting uprisings of the lower classes could not be ignored. It is not at all surprising that, in connection with the fierce dynastic conflicts that brought to an end the Julio-Claudian line of emperors, the Christians could be linked with other contemporary itinerant denouncers of the status quo and thereby be made to serve as convenient scapegoats. The successful preaching by those whom he regarded as traveling troublemakers led Pliny to inquire of Trajan as to how to handle the growing Christian movement in the remote provincial towns and countryside of Asia Minor.[44]

## V

MacMullen has also drawn attention to what will be our final type of charismatic leader, one concerning which Roman society and Roman officialdom were alternately credulous and deeply suspicious: the astrologers, diviners, and prophets.[45] In some instances, their knowledge of the future was claimed to be by divine revelation. This claim was made as well by Jewish and Christian prophets and apocalypticists, as we noted earlier in this chapter. More commonly, however, predictions of pagan seers were offered on the basis of reading the stars or the entrails of sacrificial victims (as done by augurs). The imperial reaction against the predictors of the future was not based on incredulity. To the contrary, the emperors welcomed horoscopes or prophecies that promised them long and prosperous reigns. But they profoundly feared predictions of doom, not only because such prophecies might consolidate popular opposition or withdrawal of support, but also because they feared that what was foretold might indeed come to pass. Both Jewish and Christian prophecies and apocalypses inevitably came under suspicion, as well as the predictions of pagan soothsayers, in that they all announced the end of the earthly powers and their replacement by the rule of God. The thinly veiled denunciation of the emperor in Rev. 13 could only be regarded by the imperial powers as a subversive document. All the seers who announced the impending doom of Roman sovereignty were understandably viewed as enemies of the state. Those who listened to them or transmitted their prophecies were equally guilty in the eyes of the autocratic rulers.

Each of these types of charismatic leadership is represented in the early Christian movement; each was considered to be, in MacMullen's phrase, an "enemy of Roman order." All introduced factors into Roman society that were beyond the control of the state. The seers announced the state's impending doom and saw corroborating signs in such events as comets, volcanic eruptions, unusual weather or light. The miracle workers, while bringing help to those who directly benefited from the healings and exorcisms, were regarded by skeptics as fakes. As miracle-working became increasingly associated with magic in the late second century and thereafter, the possibility of being cursed or harmed by a magician evoked fear from the highest to the lowest strata of Roman society.[46] Yet the capacity to provide leadership, whether for the objectives of health, happiness, freedom from anxiety, triumph over one's enemies, or simply to gain some sense of purpose in life, was virtually certain to elicit a ready following. What kinds of people were so eager to identify with a charismatic leader of one of the types we have sketched?

As the tradition of early Christianity portrays Jesus, he was indeed such a figure. His performances of healings and exorcisms are as firmly rooted in that tradition as is his announcement of the inbreaking of the rule of God and his summons to his disciples to leave all and follow him. Indeed, the two are linked in what is widely regarded as an authentic saying of Jesus: "If it is by the finger of God that I cast out demons, then the kingdom of God has come upon you" (Luke 11:20). In the same way the other early Christian leaders' effectiveness is linked with the miracles attributed to them and to their invitation to share in the people of the new age.[47] The compelling quality of their message was not based on rigid logic, but on the promise of dealing with human guilt, alienation, and anxiety in the face of death. What sorts of persons were ready to respond to charismatic leadership of this type? And what forms did their response take? That is the theme to which we turn next.

# 4

# PERSONAL
# AND SOCIAL IDENTITY
# IN THE NEW COMMUNITY

## I

In our discussion of the rise of charismatic leadership we touched on the preconditions which appear to be requisite for a leader of a religious movement to emerge. Chief among these necessary antecedents are (1) profound, cosmic anxiety, as a consequence of the shattering of traditional social structures, and (2) a group of followers ready to rally around the leader. This readiness may be called conversion.[1] A. D. Nock describes conversion in largely psychological terms, as "the re-orientation of the soul of the individual, his deliberate turning from indifference or from an earlier form of piety to another, a turning which implies a consciousness that the old was wrong and the new is right."[2] H. J. Mol sees conversion as "the means by which a new perspective becomes emotionally anchored in the personality, which is unified in the process."[3]

Although conversion is clearly the experience of an individual, it regularly carries with it a commitment or adherence to a new community. But that of course implies dissatisfaction with the old community. As Mol describes the process, "The convert feels that he has obtained a new identity, and very often he strengthens his new assump-

tive world by repeating over and over again how evil, or
disconsolate, or inadequate he was before the conversion
took place."[4] Obviously, the feeling of disconsolation has
subjective dimensions, but it is in large measure the product of the social setting as well. The sense of marginality
which we considered briefly in Chapter 3 was widespread
in the early years of the Roman Empire when Christianity
was coming into being and beginning its worldwide
spread. The political crisis was severe and seemingly
chronic. Even when Augustus imposed peace and order
on the Roman state, he did so at a heavy price. Traditional-
ists were upset by his overturning of the republican processes; his innovation gave larger segments of the population both status and active participation in the
decision-making. In lands dominated by imperial Rome,
age-old customs were set aside. Local regimes were either
abolished or made captive. In Palestine, Rome had imposed the half-breed Herodian dynasty on the Jews and
their Gentile neighbors. The growth of cities and mass
movements of people transplanted to populate new settle-
ments resulted in ruptures with the past, as well as in
threats to ethnic, moral, and religious roots. In Gentile
cities, the harangues of Cynic street preachers helped to
verbalize and dramatize the widespread distrust of and
disillusionment with political and religious institutions.

Ironically, the Hellenistic ambition—very nearly
brought off by Alexander—to create one world, a *cosmopolis,* increased anxieties. It was one thing to conceive
abstractly a beautiful model of the unity of the human
race; it was quite another to be set adrift in a world where
all the old grounds of identity were imperiled by agglom-
eration. Adding to the anxiety was the realization that the
masses of humanity were helpless to stem the tides of
unpredictable change or to discern meaning in the chaotic

process. Religious movements that offered a focus of identity, or a pattern of meaning, or the means for controlling one's destiny were certain to find eager prospective adherents.

## II

H. J. Mol has outlined the process of conversion in an illuminating way. The first stage is what he calls "detachment from former patterns of identity."[5] This could take the form of turning back to a widely held tradition, which had been abandoned earlier out of skepticism, or it could be a turning to a new form of religion as Nock suggests.[6] It could be the outcome of a process of disillusionment, or it could come in more cataclysmic fashion. The rise of Pharisaism seems to be a case of the former type. Disillusioned with the national and religious leadership of the Jewish people in the Maccabean period, the leaders of the Pharisaic movement withdrew from direct political involvement and quietly launched an enterprise consisting of small groups meeting privately for study of the legal traditions of Israel. From that corporate study they drew guidelines that would enable their members to live in their present circumstances in obedience to their tradition. More dramatic was the withdrawal from society by the followers of the Teacher of Righteousness, which is reflected in the Dead Sea community's Manual of Discipline and the so-called Damascus Document. In the opening lines of the latter writing we can read how the community at Qumran understood itself to have been brought into existence by God:

They perceived their iniquity and knew that they were guilty men; yet they were like men blind and groping for the way for twenty years. And God observed their works, that they sought him with a perfect heart; and he raised up for them a teacher of righteousness to lead them in the way of his heart.

The document goes on to describe how the leaders of Israel had betrayed their heritage, "so that they turn aside from the paths of righteousness. . . . They sought smooth things, and chose illusions . . . they transgressed the covenant and violated the statute." Thus the only way God could accomplish his purpose was to raise up a faithful remnant, who would be the agents through whom the true people of God would arise. He anointed them with "his holy Spirit and a revelation of truth . . . to see and understand the works of God, and to choose what he likes and reject what he hates, to walk perfectly in all his ways."[7] These revelations are addressed to "all those who have entered the covenant"; that is, those who have abandoned their old ways and old leadership to cast their lot with the people of the new covenant.

Similarly, those addressed by John the Baptist are instructed to abandon their present claims to be children of Abraham (Luke 3:8) and to adopt a new pattern of life in expectation of the divine judgment. The outward dramatic sign of the inward change was baptism in the Jordan, an aspect of conversion to which we shall turn later in this chapter. Jesus and his followers are attracted by John's call to repentance, according to the Gospel tradition, and according to the early Christian preaching incorporated in the sermons of Acts (Acts 10:37).

Jesus' call to his followers includes a break with the past. The disciples James and John left the family fishing business in the hands of their father and the hired servants (Mark 1:20). Jesus encountered rejection in his own home town (Mark 6:1–6), and came to be regarded as mad by his own family (Mark 3:21).[8] The necessity of a break with one's family is explicit in Mark 3:31, and in the rebuke to the would-be disciple who wanted to return home to meet his family obligations (Luke 9:60–62). Indeed the family is redefined as those who do the will of God (Mark 3:35), in direct contrast to the earthly family.

Paul's account of his conversion (Gal. 1:11–17) begins with an enumeration of the acts of zeal with which he had formerly sought to destroy the church, to whose welfare and growth his energies and existence are now wholly dedicated. Similarly, in Phil. 3 he lists those things he had formerly counted as values (ritual purity, tribal lineage, legal training, zeal as a defender of the truth), all of which he now characterizes as excrement (Phil. 3:8). His identity and his values have been exchanged for a new goal: to gain Christ and to be found "in him" (Phil. 3:9), with a new standing before God and a new hope for life beyond death.

Acts is strewn with conversion accounts, which highlight the radical nature of the change—culturally and in terms of social identity—when the gospel is heard and believed: those who experience this transformation come on the scene in Acts as a Roman centurion, a jailer in Philippi, a businesswoman from Thyatira, to say nothing of the lame, blind, and diseased who are healed and the magicians and mediums who are converted.

The excerpt quoted above from the Damascus Document mentions the factor that Mol sees as the second stage in conversion: the situation of meaninglessness and anomie.[9] This dimension is scarcely even implicit in the New Testament accounts of John the Baptist or Jesus, or in the letters of Paul, but it is present in the conversion accounts of Acts. Paul wanders about blind; the Ethiopian eunuch is returning home from his pilgrimage to Jerusalem perplexed by what he reads in the Jewish Scriptures; Peter's "conversion" to support for the Christian mission to Gentiles comes only after a puzzling vision of a kind of zoo in a heavenly handkerchief (Acts 10–11), and it has to be repeated three times before he gets the point. Paul writes that the light shines "out of darkness" (II Cor. 4:6). John the Evangelist likewise (John 1:5) observes that it is in the midst of the human condition of darkness that the light of God comes to those prepared to receive it (John 1:11–12).

The dramatic moment of transition from darkness to light, from chaos to meaning, is Mol's third stage in conversion.[10] In the Gospel tradition, the symbolic action is a voice from heaven, and the Spirit descending like a dove. For Paul it is the revelation of the risen Jesus (Gal. 1:16; I Cor. 15:8). According to Acts 9, it was a light from heaven and the voice of Jesus that brought Paul to Christian faith. The importance and the appeal of the story for purposes of Christian propaganda among seeking Gentiles is evident in its being repeated twice (Acts 22 and 26) as a part of Paul's defense before civil authorities. Pagan literature of the period likewise reports the astonishing accompaniments of the conversion of persons to become followers of a savior-divinity. Apuleius, in his *Metamorphoses,* depicts with vivid detail the apparition of Isis to the bewitched hero. Rising from the sea, she comes to bless her devotee, to release him from his curse (he had been transformed into an ass) by restoring his authentic humanity, to address him and instruct him concerning the ceremonies in which his further transformation will occur, and to promise him eternal life in her presence.

A. J. Festugière, in his study *Epicurus and His Gods,* summarizes the account preserved by a poet (perhaps Menander, ca. 342–ca. 291 B.C.) in which a young man describes his conversion: his previous life was a living death, but now the darkness has been removed. He compares his

experience with that of one who slept in the temple of
Asclepius and awoke healed, restored, saved.[11] The implication is that this conversion is of a kind with those under-
gone by young persons who commit themselves to the
circle of friends that surrounded Epicurus. The analogy is
not completely inappropriate. Indeed, the final step in the
conversion experience comes in the actions of the community by which they support and accept into their group the
initiate.[12] That comes through in Apuleius' account; after
he has been changed back into truly human form, other
devotees of Isis offer him clothing and share with him in
the sacred meal. Similarly, the newly converted Saul/Paul
(Acts 9) is addressed by a leader of the Damascus Christian
community as "Brother Saul" and is baptized and fed,
remaining for some time with the other Christians there.
On his arrival in Jerusalem, he is recognized as the chief
persecutor of the church and feared, but by divine instruction he is received by the Jerusalem Christians and then
sent on his way to his native territory. Paul does not mention this visit at the time of his conversion, but he was
offered hospitality later by the leading Jerusalem-based
apostles (Gal. 1:18) and given the "right hand of fellow-
ship" (Gal. 2:9), which was a sign of acceptance and mutual
trust.

In a book significantly titled *The God That Failed,* Arthur Koestler described the experience of escape from his
confused and conflict-ridden past into the light of the com-
munist world view. He said that "the whole universe [fell]
into pattern like the stray pieces of a jigsaw puzzle assembled by magic at one stroke."[13] The effects of the conversion wore off, of course, but for our purposes it is important
to discern the initial psychological impact of the experience, as well as the new cosmos or life world and the social
identity which are thereby established. Broadly speaking,

the pattern of conversion is by no means unique to Christianity, as we have noted above.

Rather than assuming simple identities between pagan and early Christian phenomena of conversion, however, it is essential to discern how different are the groups into which conversion occurred, and to recognize that these differences are linked with the life world that each group represents or espouses. The Epicureans, for example, rejected political involvement of any kind, turning rather to "the intimate hearth of the inner life."[14] Epicurean ethics has been characterized as "the internalization of ethics by the exaltation of the role of feelings over reason."[15] Happiness is the goal of existence, and it lies in peace of mind, free of the limiting attachment to desires of any kind. Even the study of nature is justified only on the ground that it will overcome fear of natural catastrophe, and thereby contribute to the tranquillity of the soul. For this state of mind the presence of, and interchange with, others of like persuasion was essential, and respect for all other human beings was enjoined. But the ancient symbol of the Epicureans, while wholly fitting for that movement, is unsuitable for nascent Christianity: the Garden, the safe retreat from the difficulties of life for the elite "family," who were truly self-sufficient.[16] Conversion to such a group, while similar in form to that of the early Christians, stands in sharpest contrast to Christian conversion with its conviction of the impending end of the age and its commitment to spread the good news by word and act so that as many as possible would be ready to enter the kingdom of God.

## III

One of the most striking features of religion in the Hellenistic period is that participation was a voluntary matter. In the modern Western world voluntarism is unsurprising, but in the ancient world that factor was a novelty. In his epochal study *The Ancient City,* N. D. Fustel de Coulanges showed how central for identity in very early Rome (prior to the founding of the republic) was a family, with its hearth as the prime focus of religion; continuity of identity was provided by the ongoing existence of the family through successive generations.[17] Although the state replaced the family as the center of social identity in the days of the republic,[18] the new laws preserved the power of the father. In the imperial period emperors sought to authenticate their chosen successors by adopting them legally as sons, and claimants to the imperial seat claimed to be in the paternal succession.

From the republican period of Rome onward, craftsmen and those attached to the cult of various divinities formed voluntary associations called *collegia,* which were occasionally outlawed because they could exercise considerable power. They were not unlike labor unions or lobbying blocs today. But these associations seem to have been formed for specific and limited purposes: to foster the common welfare of a craft, or to honor appropriately a divine benefactor (such as Asclepius) or benefactress (such as Isis). Although Nock suggests the possibility that there were organized communities behind some of the cults of the later Roman empire,[19] the evidence is ambiguous, as he acknowledges. Even under the empire the welfare of the state, *res publica,* was the central value for Rome. Religion of a public sort was patterned after the household worship, with the *cella* of a temple replacing the hearth, but the worship was now directed to the prosperity and stability of the state, rather than to the family or tribe. Private religion and small cult groups offered no threat to that civil stability. Writers like Juvenal heaped scorn on those who became adherents of the oriental divinities, however. In his *Satires,* Juvenal scoffs at the motivation for joining such groups ("bribed no doubt by a fat goose and a slice of sacrificial cake") and sneers at the conduct of the worship ("the chorus of the frantic Bellona and the Mother of the Gods, attended by a giant eunuch to whom his obscene inferiors must do reverence").[20]

It is impossible at a remove of two millennia to be certain as to what sorts of persons were appealed to by these cults. In the Roman port of Ostia by the second century A.D. there were scores of shrines and cult centers, dedicated not only to traditional Roman deities and to "Roma and Augustus," but also to Syrian, Phrygian, and Egyptian deities. More inscriptions and dedications to Isis were found at Ostia than at any other place in the Roman world. There were at least six shrines of Mithras.[21] L. R. Taylor thinks that the chief devotees were "ex-slaves and descendants of slaves of oriental stock."[22] That may be the case, but the traditional gods seem, broadly speaking, to have lost their hold on popular affection and devotion. The shrines of Roma and Augustus provided a focus for a kind of civil religion, in which the founder of the empire was venerated and hopes for political stability were expressed; it may be significant that shrines of this kind were found in all the major port cities of Italy, including Ostia, which was the greatest port of its day.[23] But the dynastic shifts and the mental incompetence of some who sat in the imperial chair in the first century must have produced a profound sense of unease and uncertainty that could not be assuaged or overcome by the traditional gods or by a contrived, compulsory imperial cult. The oriental divinities must have exercized a broad appeal. As J. Carcopino wrote in his classic *Daily Life in Ancient Rome:*

> These are the deities who, far from being impassive, suffer, die, and rise from the dead; gods whose myths embrace the cosmos and comprehend its secrets; gods whose astral fatherland dominates all earthly fatherlands and who assure to their initiates alone, but to them without distinction of nationality or status, a protection proportionate to the purity of each.[24]

It is precisely the appeal across barriers of family, ethnic origin, and social status that aroused the hopes of the alienated as well as the anxieties of the privileged. Although the Roman establishment on the whole regarded these cultic movements with mingled disdain and hostility, there were various modes of propaganda that attracted numbers of people who felt themselves to be marginal, as Nock has pointed out. The cults grew through personal testimony of individuals who had experienced deliverance ("salvation") from sickness or fear or both, through literary apologies (although these were probably minimally effective); through public ceremonies and confessions by penitents; through public inscriptions at shrines of healing gods, bearing witness to their transforming power.[25] Even the attack by Lucian of Samosata on the miracle worker Alexander of Abonuteichos—whom Lucian portrays as a charlatan—gives evidence of the public nature and broad appeal of miracle and ritual.[26] No longer overwhelmed or led to quiet despair by a sense of being driven to an inescapable fate or of being hemmed in by insurmountable limits, individuals were convinced that their decisions mattered. The choices they made could contribute to the determination of their destiny. But what would lead the religious seeker to a particular choice among the many options that were open for gaining access to the secrets of the cosmos and for achieving identity and purpose in a fragmented and seemingly unpredictable world?

## IV

The contender that attained the greatest success in propagation of its way of salvation was one that on the surface seemed an unlikely candidate: Christianity. Down into the second century, it was a relatively obscure movement. Pliny had to write to Trajan (98–117) for instructions about dealing with this odd sect called Christians. He had to probe and threaten in order to find out even what they did in their religious gatherings, and the results were scarcely worth the effort, so banal and bland did they sound:

> They were in the habit of meeting on a certain fixed day before it was light, when they sang in alternate verses a hymn to Christ as to a god, and bound themselves by solemn oath—not to do any wicked deeds, but never to commit any fraud, theft or adultery, never to falsify their word, nor deny a trust when they should be called upon to deliver it up; after which it was their custom to separate, and then to reassemble to partake of food—but food of an ordinary and innocent kind.[27]

He goes on to mention "depraved and excessive superstition," but offers no details. In short, Christian sectarian gatherings sound like a blend of simple liturgy, humanitarian ethics, and a church supper. Scarcely exceptional, but not exceptionable, either. The sole serious charge that Pliny is able to bring, and that is echoed in Trajan's response, is that the Christians refused under penalty of death to participate in divine honors to "our gods"; that is, to the gods upon whose favor depended the welfare of the Roman state.

Celsus, one of Christianity's most effective intellectual critics, who flourished during the reign of Hadrian (117–138), scoffed at the movement as low-class. It invited scoundrels and crooks to its meetings, rejoiced in its lack of worldly wisdom, and met in shops run by ignorant craftsmen.[28] His assessment was not entirely accurate, but of course it served his purposes to draw attention to the most blatant counter-cultural features. As early as the time of Paul, the church in Corinth included among its members some persons of at least modest achievement in Roman society, as we shall consider shortly. But it is probably significant that the most likely site of a Christian gathering place that has yet been found among the ruins of ancient Corinth is a little shop on the main street that leads down to the port from the center of the city, the ancient equivalent of a storefront church.[29]

What was it that brought such diverse and ever-increasing groups of people together in the Christian communities? It was primarily the Christians' version of the Jewish concept of covenant people. In the original Jewish concept of covenant, there was first of all a sense *of divine destiny*. The God of Israel had chosen Abraham, Isaac, Jacob, and their posterity to be the recipients of his revealed law, to be the guardians of the sanctuary where he chose to dwell among them on Mount Zion and—at least in the prophetic strand of the Jewish tradition—to be "a light to the nations" (Isa. 42:6), so that all mankind would ultimately have the opportunity to share in God's grace through his people Israel. That sense of destiny reached back into the past, as well: the seeming catastrophes of enslavement in Egypt and later the captivity in Babylon were seen as the occasion for acts of divine deliverance, which confirmed Israel's covenant status before its God.

As a people who had entered into covenant relationship with God on Mount Sinai, and in subsequent acts of covenant renewal, Israel was able to deal positively with a second crucial factor: *the problem of evil.* There is no single solution to this perennial question in the Jewish Scriptures; indeed, certain of the Scriptures are frankly skeptical (Ecclesiastes) or so doubt-ridden that the writer finally takes refuge in a mystery (Job). But there is a persistent theme maintaining that suffering is redemptive, and that Israel is God's servant chosen to suffer in the fulfillment of His purpose (Second Isaiah). The latest portions of the prophetic writings, and especially Daniel, regarded the present suffering of the covenant people as the final stage in God's act of deliverance: the birthpangs of the new age. The problem of life after death is no more than hinted at in the Hebrew Scriptures.[30] Only in the later Jewish writings in Greek (especially the Wisdom of Solomon) does there appear the concept of the immortality of the soul. The dominant hope is for the survival and prosperity of the covenant people, as in the blessings pronounced on the posterity of Abraham (Gen. 17:20–21).

Yet there was no general agreement throughout Judaism as to who would share in the covenant promises. Although the older Jewish tradition affirmed that the nations of the world would share in the blessings to Abraham, the mode of participation was vague and Gentiles were not permitted to become members of the covenant people. In Hellenistic times,[31] Gentiles were admitted to the covenant community. Proselytes, as they were called, were presumably first given instruction, and then required to accept circumcision and baptism.[32] Others who were not ready to take these steps were permitted to share in the synagogue worship. In spite of scholarly disagreement

whether designations used in Acts, such as "devout persons" (Acts 17:17) or "[female] worshiper of God" (Acts
16:14), were technical terms for Gentiles on the fringes of
Judaism, the terms do indicate a degree of openness toward Gentiles among Jews in predominantly Gentile centers, as well as the keen interest of Gentiles in the strictly
monotheistic, highly moral, aniconic Jewish religion.
Nevertheless, Gentiles remained marginal to the covenant life. Since circumcision was essential for proselytes,
it is not clear whether women were able to become members of the covenant people, although some grave inscriptions bear the feminine term, *proselyta*, which implies
equal status. From the accounts in Acts, however, we can
infer that it was among proselytes and Gentile worshipers
of Israel's God that the Christian missionaries found their
best prospects for conversion to the new faith.

The reasons for that are readily apparent. Paul stated
succinctly what in his view was uniquely appealing about
the new covenant people, for which he employs the mystical shorthand term "in Christ." Christ is understood to be
the founder and locus of the new people of God:

> For in Christ Jesus you are all sons of God, through faith. For
> as many of you as were baptized into Christ have put on
> Christ. There is neither Jew nor Greek, there is neither
> slave nor free, there is neither male nor female; for you are
> all one in Christ Jesus. And if you are Christ's, then you are
> Abraham's offspring, heirs according to promise. (Gal. 3:
> 26–29)

All the social, ethnic, traditional-religious, and sexual dif
ferences that dominated the Roman world have been
eliminated or transcended in the new covenant community. Not only the pious Gentile, hovering on the fringes
of Judaism, but any person of whatever sex or race, whatever social or economic status, was at least potentially

welcome in this inclusive people of God.

In contrast to views dominant in Greco-Roman culture, the New Testament writers manifest a relatively open attitude toward women—a factor that seems to have contributed significantly to the rapid growth of the early Christian movement. Ironically, Paul has been accused of holding antifeminine views, as in his placing women in a position of seeming subservience to their husbands (I Cor. 11:3). But in relation to the culture of the Roman world, Christian women seem to have been given wider opportunities and to have been accorded a position far closer to equality with men than was the case in other human associations of the time. Fustel de Coulanges has shown that a Roman woman never had a hearth or worship of her own, never exercised authority in relation to worship, was never free or mistress of herself, and at her husband's death ceased to be the *mater familias*. He recalls the evidence from Plutarch that women could not appear in court as witnesses, and from Gaius (late second century A.D.) "that nothing can be granted in the way of justice to persons under power—that is to say, to wives, sons, slaves."[33] When the senate wished to root out the worship of Bacchus, with its wild excesses as they had earlier been depicted in Euripides' *Bacchae,* it concluded reluctantly that it must turn over the task of judging them to the sole traditional authority over women: their husbands. As Cato the Elder put it: "His power has no limit; he can do [with his wife] what he chooses."[34]

In sharp contrast to this widespread Roman attitude toward women is the theoretical equality that is theirs in the people of the new covenant and the actual roles of leadership that they seem to have filled from the outset of the movement. This is evident in the Gospel tradition; for example, the redefined "family" in Mark 3:34–35 includes

mother and sisters as well as brothers. The oldest documented stage of tradition concerning Jesus' teaching on
divorce (Mark 10:2–9) establishes a mutuality of responsibility that contrasts with the Jewish legal provision for the
husband to divorce his wife unilaterally. The private comment of Jesus (Mark 10:10–12), even though it may represent a somewhat later development of the tradition, is
significant in that it presupposes for the woman fully
equivalent rights in divorce and remarriage.

The initiative of women in coming to Jesus for help and
their participation in the community of faith is occasionally reported in Mark, but it is a theme that is expanded
somewhat in Q and that becomes a major factor in Luke.
The fidelity of the women is attested in Mark and Q, as is
their share in eschatological conflict. But in Luke, the role
of women is highlighted, both throughout the Gospel and
in the Acts. Women are the recipients of the heavenly
revelation about the birth of Jesus and his forerunner, as
well as the divinely prepared agents by which Jesus and
John come into the human realm. The ecstatic hymns by
which John and Jesus are hailed at their advent, according
to Luke, are uttered by women. The witnesses in Jesus'
behalf at the time of his presentation in Jerusalem included the prophetess Anna (Luke 2:36–38). More than is
the case in Mark, women in Luke take the initiative in
coming to Jesus to be healed or forgiven (Luke 7:11–17;
13:10–17). They organize support for Jesus (8:1–3); they
care for his needs and are more open to his teachings
(10:38–42). They are featured in his parables (15:8–10).
They are highly audible among his followers (11:27–28).
They stand by him faithfully from the launching of his
work in Galilee until his death in Jerusalem (23:27–31, 55),
for which they are rewarded by seeing the empty tomb
and receiving the first report of Jesus' resurrection.

The importance of women for the early Christian mission is reported in detail in Acts. From the Scripture quoted to interpret the outpouring of the Spirit on Pentecost, which attests that men *and* women will prophesy and will receive the Spirit, women share with men in the leadership of the church (Acts 12:12; 16:1, 14; 18:2, 19), in persecution (9:2; 22:4), in proportion of converts (5:14; 17:34), in welfare distribution (6:1), and in support for the apostles (21:5). The New Testament evidence is not sufficient to say that there was full equality between the sexes —for example, all the twelve disciples are male—but the prominence given to women is an unusual feature of social movements of the early empire. From the inscriptions and the literary sources providing information on the cult of Isis, for example, as well as from the pictorial representations of the cult (as in the Iseum at Pompeii), we may conclude that women were initiated into the mystery of Isis, but it is clear that their official participation in the cult was auxiliary to that of the male priesthood. The priestess is pictured standing beside the high priest; women play musical instruments or strew flowers in the path of the Isiac processions, but theirs is clearly a subsidiary role. In the pre-Christian era, Euripides was scathingly critical of the women devotees of Dionysus; in the days of the Roman republic, Livy reports (*History of Rome,* Book XXXIX) that women were the chief instigators of the Bacchanalia, the nocturnal ceremonial orgies that resulted in murders and every manner of sexual excess. Thus women's roles in religious movements were widely suspect in the days of the early empire. The Christian movement challenged that attitude and provided women with new forms of religious participation.

The open attitude toward persons considered outsiders by Jewish standards permeates both the Gospels and the letters of Paul, and it is a central theme in Acts as well. In both Markan (Mark 2:15) and Q tradition (Matt. 11:19; Luke 7:34–35), Jesus is depicted as attracting tax collectors and sinners, persons who would be rejected by pious Jews on moral, ritual, or patriotic grounds. Luke shows Jesus selecting as one of his disciples a tax collector in Jericho (Luke 19:1–10); commending the compassion shown by a hated Samaritan (Luke 10:29–37); and portraying God in the image of a father who rejoices in the return of a wastrel son. Paul stakes his entire apostleship on the issue of a controversy in which he maintained that Gentile converts are not to be held to the demands of the Jewish law (Galatians 1–3). The redefinition of the covenant community as an inclusive body is the major theme of the most systematic of Paul's writings, the letter to the Romans:

> That is why it depends on faith, in order that the promise may rest on grace and be guaranteed to all his descendants —not only to the adherents of the law but also to those who share the faith of Abraham, for he is the father of us all, as it is written, "I have made you the father of many nations." (Rom. 4:16–17)

Acts reinforces this image of the universality of the new community, from the worldwide representation at the outpouring of the Spirit in Acts 2; through the conversion of representatives of various nations (Ethiopians, Samaritans, Romans, Greeks); the vision of Peter (Acts 10) with the menagerie in the celestial sheet; and the successive narratives of the spread of the gospel through the urban centers of Syria, Anatolia, and the Aegean, moving from the center of the Jewish world to the capital of the empire. As Paul phrased it, "In Christ God was reconciling the *cosmos* to himself" (II Cor 5:19).

The concept of the covenant community as a new people seems to have exercised a peculiar appeal in the first century of the church's existence. Paul clearly differentiated Jews/Greeks/church (I Cor. 10:32). Leadership in the new covenant people was regarded by Paul as the ground of human freedom, of access into the glorious presence of God and thereby into true knowledge of God (II Cor. 3:4–6, 12–18; 4:3–6). Participation was not by fulfillment of a killing code of regulations, but by acceptance in faith of divine grace conveyed by the Spirit of God.

V

The idealized picture of the unified community of the covenant did not, unfortunately, correspond wholly to the empirical situation of primitive Christianity. The tensions and conflicts are apparent in the letters of Paul, tensions between Paul and the other apostles and conflicts within the local congregations. In part, at least, these conflicts were sociological in nature, although they were perceived by those involved as primarily theological differences. The issue of the degree of inclusiveness of the Christian community was precisely the cause of conflict between vacillating Peter and adamant Paul in the Antioch incident heatedly reported by Paul in Gal. 1–2. The same problem of the relationships between membership in the old and new covenant communities surfaces in II Cor. 11:22, where he responds with bitter sarcasm to those who have challenged his credentials as apostle. Apparently those who called into question Paul's apostolic authority in the churches he had founded, including the one at Corinth (I Cor. 12:27–30) made boast of their ecstatic gifts: prophecy, miracle-working, speaking in tongues, healing. Without denying that these capabilities were the gifts of the Spirit, Paul pleads that "all things should be done decently and in order" (I Cor. 14:40). He is worried about what visitors will think when they see these unbridled ecstatic manifestations: "Will they not say that you are mad?" (I Cor. 14:23).

What seems to be at the root of the conflict between Paul and the other apostles is a fundamental difference in social conception of the church and its corporate life. The ecstatics probably stood in the tradition described in the Gospels (Mark 3; Matt. 10; Luke 6), where Jesus is reported to have sent out his disciples as itinerant preachers and wonder workers. As they moved from village to village, living from hospitality offered them on the way, their model is closer to the Cynic preachers than to the organized urban congregations that show up in Paul's letters. In the structured city congregations, the authority of Paul was to be recognized for settling disputes, even in his absence (I Cor. 5:4–5).

In sharp contrast to the structure and order of the Pauline-founded congregations are the communities established and sustained by wandering charismatics. Gerd Theissen has developed a detailed and, on the whole, convincing picture of this phenomenon, which he calls "the Jesus movement."[35] He proposes that the three essential ingredients in this movement were "the wandering charismatics, their sympathizers in the local communities, and the bearer of revelation." These stood in complementary relationship to each other; the charismatics were the spiritual authorities for the communities; the communities provided the material support and the social context for the work of the charismatics; "both owed their existence and legitimation to the transcendent bearer of revelation."[36] Cut off from all ordinary human obligations (home, family, income), they announced the end of the age; to them flocked "the crippled, prostitutes and good-for-nothings, tax collectors and prodigal sons."[37] The critique of wealth and possessions, the call to homelessness and joblessness could only be regarded by outsiders (i.e., both non-Christians and Christian non-charismatics) as at best irresponsible and at worst subversive of civil order. Their ethical demands were based on sayings of Jesus, or declarations made in his name, as the I-style and the juridical pronouncements in his name indicate (Mark 8:38; Matt. 10:40).[38] Both the importance of hospitality to the wanderers and the fact that these regulations arose in the post-Jesus stage of the tradition seems clear from Mark 9:41: "For truly, I say to you, whoever gives you a cup of water to drink because you bear the name of Christ, will by no means lose his reward."

This spontaneity of movement and the charismatic basis of ethical instruction is a sociological world far removed from the Pauline atmosphere, where all things are to be done "decently and in order" (I Cor. 14:40). If Colossians is an authentic letter of Paul, then we have an instance of his using the so-called *Haustafel,* or table of household rules, with its guidelines for the behavior of the community membership, and instruction in detail for wives and husbands, slaves and masters (Col. 3–4).[39] But even if Colossians is regarded as pseudepigraphic, two observations are warranted: (1) The letter stands closer to Paul than do any other of the deutero-Pauline writings, and on social and ethical issues there is substantive agreement with the genuine Pauline writings. (2) The Pauline letters, even though they lack the specific format of the *Haustafel,* are profoundly and pervasively concerned with the internal ordering of the communities, in a manner which is not discernible at all in the Q tradition, for example. Paul exercises his apostolic authority in laying down rules on such matters as the public image of the church (I Cor. 5:1;

6:6; 7:35; 10:32), due process based on submission to su-
periors within the church (I Cor. 9–10; 12:14–31), avoidance of conflict with civil authorities (Rom. 13), and careful
administration of finances (I Cor. 16). There are, of course,
charismatic gifts evident in the Pauline churches, as there
seem to have been in the community that lies behind Q,
but Paul finds these gifts problematical or even an embar-
rassment, ego-inflating, and a constant source of confusion
and of a bad public image. Even the charismatic gifts, he
decrees, are to be administered in an orderly way (I Cor.
14:20–33): "God is not a God of disorder but of peace." It
is no wonder, therefore, that representatives of these two
very different approaches to what we might today call
"Christian life-style" would provoke personal and ideolog-
ical conflicts. Paul's involuted arguments in I and II Corinthians seem to be his attempt simultaneously to distance
himself from the unstructured behavior of the charismatics and to affirm the reality of his own conversion experience and apostolic role.

Even within the urban congregations, however, there
were social tensions, stemming in large measure from the
inclusiveness of the message that had attracted adherents
in the first place, resulting from social and cultural differences within a single congregation. This factor is clearest
in the letters of Paul. For example, in Rom. 16:23 Paul
extends greetings from the church in Corinth to the
church in Rome, which he had not yet visited, but in
which he obviously knew many persons. Perhaps these
personal links were the result merely of travel for business
reasons, but according to Acts 18:2, some Christians, notably Aquila and Priscilla, found their way to Corinth after
Claudius drove the Jews—and apparently the Christians as
well—from Rome. Later this couple sent greetings back to
Corinth from Ephesus (I Cor. 16:19), and now they are

back in Rome. One gets the impression of Paul's constituents as including persons of economic substance and cosmopolitan culture.

Paul wrote that there were not "many" of the wise, the noble, and the powerful in the church at Corinth (I Cor. 1:26); he does not say there are not *any* of the upper socioeconomic and cultural levels. Theissen has suggested that they were a "dominant minority."[40] At any rate, they included the city treasurer of Corinth and a certain Gaius, whose quarters were sufficiently spacious to provide hospitality for Paul and the whole church. There is an implication that Paul's detractors were condescending to him because he worked with his hands to make a living (I Cor. 9:6), as he himself expressly says in I Cor. 4:12. In the same context he contrasts his own miserable clothing, inferior economic status, and social impotence with that of his well-heeled, socially powerful critics. The words he uses to describe himself and his immediate associates are the first-century equivalent of "scum" and "trash" (I Cor. 4:13). Theissen proposes that the group vaguely referred to as "Chloe's people" (I Cor. 1:11), who have reported to Paul the quarreling that is dividing the church in Corinth, may themselves have been from the lower strata.[41]

Paul seeks to show that he regards the work of Apollos as complementary to his own (I Cor. 3:5–6), even though, as may be inferred from I Cor. 3:18–22 and 4:6–7, Apollos had become the darling of the "wise" contingent in the Corinthian church. If the detail about Apollos in Acts 18:24 is accurate, he was a cultured person, presumably instructed in the Alexandrine method of scriptural interpretation best known from the works of Philo of Alexandria, whose allegorical exegesis was based on Platonic and Stoic philosophy. Yet Paul, the Syrian hand laborer, and Apollos, the Alexandrian man of culture, had in common not only their common faith but also their common efforts in behalf of the Christian mission in the commercial and cultural crossroads that was Corinth.

The problems of internal social tensions plagued the church from the outset and continued to do so in the postapostolic period. In the second century the church began to occupy itself with such questions as ecclesiastical order and unity of doctrine. But from the outset, a prior problem was how to actualize the social unity of the church that very early spanned so wide a range of economic, social, and cultural strata. By the end of the first century there may have been converts to Christianity in the imperial household itself, as we may infer from the fact that Domitian's persecution of "atheists" in A.D. 95[42] resulted in the death of his co-consul Flavius Clemens and the exile of the latter's wife Domitilla. By the very attractiveness of its inclusive concept of covenant community, the church set for itself the problem of blending into one society members whose backgrounds were as diverse as village hand craftsmen, women of wealth and prestigious families, minor Roman officers, social and moral outcasts, persons with rhetorical and philosophical training, some reared in strict Jewish legal environments, and others who were "ordinary men of no education" (Acts 4:13, TEV). For such a socially diverse group to achieve a sense of unity required far more than mere social adjustment on a person-to-person basis. In striving for unity, stability, numerical expansion, and upward social mobility, Christians had to find ways by which to adapt their traditions and to develop them in ways that might enhance the movement's appeal. The process was complex. It is to that subject we now move.

# 5

# CULT AND CULTURE

A revealing aspect of the "one world" ideal promoted by Alexander and his successors was the urge to assert the essential oneness behind the multiplicity of names for gods and goddesses. The aim was not monotheism, in the sense of affirming the sole existence of a single deity, but rather syncretism, which sought to demonstrate the hypothetical unity which supposedly underlay the diversity of modes of worship in the Greco-Roman world. Classic evidence of the syncretistic intent is found in the address by Isis to Apuleius at the climax of his initiation. She explains that various peoples call her by different names: Mother of Gods (Phrygia), Minerva (Athens), Venus (Cyprus), Diana (Crete), Prosperpine (Sicily), Ceres (Eleusis); elsewhere she is variously known as Juno Bellona, Hecate, Rhamnusia. But her real name is Isis.[1] In an increasingly mobile society, where military or business demands moved large segments of the populace around the Mediterranean world, it was to the advantage of both local priests and newly arrived worshipers to be able to find a familiar divinity behind the unaccustomed exterior or titles in strange surroundings. For the philosophically inclined theorists, of course, there was the added value of discerning the one deity behind the many manifestations.

The blending of religious traditions is apparent in the narrative of Acts 19. There Paul and his colleagues come in conflict with the priesthood of the temple of Artemis at Ephesus, with the souvenir makers who benefit from the tourist and pilgrim trade that came to her justly renowned shrine, and with the populace devoted to her as their patron goddess. Although she had long been known as Artemis of the Ephesians, her origins are almost certainly linked with the Asian Great Mother tradition, as her image with multiple breasts confirms. Furthermore, she was represented at her shrine in Ephesus—in addition to the many-breasted image found on coins from Ephesus and probably exhibited in her temple—by a meteorite. Meteorites were placed as well in shrines of the Great Mother at Troy and at Pessinus in Phrygia (later transferred to her temple in Rome).[2] There can be no doubt that syncretistic influences were at work in the development of the Christian tradition, as they were in the pagan cults. Christianity's absorption and adaptation of older religious elements is tangibly evident in some of the early churches, such as that of San Clemente in Rome, where the high altar is built directly over a shrine of Mithras, or in Bethlehem, where Jerome tells us that there was on the site of Jesus' birth a grove and shrine sacred to Venus and Adonis. Why, then, did not Christianity simply blend in with the other Eastern cults? Should not a sect that stressed so strongly its inclusiveness have assimilated itself to other outwardly similar cultic movements?

I

In responding to the questions just posed, we must first look at the stages in the development of sacred identity and do so in general, theoretical terms. As we have noted,

Mol has outlined what he calls "four mechanisms of the sacralization process on both the personal and the social level." They are (1) objectification, (2) commitment, (3) ritual, and (4) myth.[3] In the earlier chapters of this book we have sketched two of these social functions: the construction of the sacred cosmos (objectification) and the dynamic between a charismatic leader and the religious movement that develops around him (commitment). In the remaining two factors, myth and ritual, lie the forces that provide the community with its sense of ongoing history as well as with its group identity. Myth and ritual are not fixed patterns or stereotypes, but dynamic processes of adaptation and renewal of social and conceptual structures in the changing conditions of the community's existence.

This process of adaptation of myth and cult has been called "structural transformation," as described by Jean Piaget in his *Structuralism*.[4] Piaget has conceived it in a mode importantly different from the structuralist method associated with Claude Lévi-Strauss.[5] The structuralists who follow Lévi-Strauss—which is to say, the vast majority who thus designate themselves—are, like him, not really interested in the variety of cultural phenomena that seemingly differentiate one culture from another with regard to myth, ritual, and social institutions. Rather, their focus is on the "deep structures" within the human mind that are said to be common to all human beings. In Lévi-Strauss's view, attention to surface features, such as historical origins and influences, obscures the underlying essence. In the matter of linguistics, the orthodox structuralist has no interest in historical or genetic questions about language development, but concentrates rather on the universal feature of contrasting pairs (hot/cold, up/down, in/out, etc.), which Lévi-Strauss has called "binary opposition."[6] This linguistic quality is then used as a device to account for all aspects of culture and society. Since language is the expression of thought, according to Lévi-Strauss, the human mind functions in every age and culture by binary opposition.

Anthropologists who continue to be concerned with the analysis of discrete and different cultural phenomena have not been persuaded by this grandiose pattern of universal thought. In obvious reference to Lévi-Strauss's work in which his theory was set forth, *The Raw and the Cooked*,[7] K. O. L. Burridge has remarked: "Like the children who followed the pied piper, once caught by the jogging beat of binary oppositions, enthusiasts may jump for joy, not caring whether the next meal is raw or cooked. . . . Lévi-Strauss' method seems to impose a spurious uniformity on the material, spurious because order springs not from the encounter between investigator and data but from the categories of a closed system, which cannot admit further possibilities. It negates the whole task of discovering the different kinds of forms within which the same sets of relations are organized or given coherence."[8]

Some biblical scholars have sought to make exegetical use of Straussian structuralist methods, especially in France and to a lesser degree in America.[9] The results of exegesis on this hypothetical basis are largely common-places or allegorization or both. For example, Jean Starobinski's analysis of Mark 5:1–20, the story of the Gerasene demoniac, dismisses historical and cultural dimensions of the narrative and takes refuge in a "parabolic" approach that locates the story in the "depths of subjectivity," where the "surface narrative" is replaced by a "psychic event."[10] This interpretative process—which is supposed to be concerned with the text alone and entire,[11] calls itself "parabolic" and deplores allegorical interpretation,

but is finally indistinguishable from allegory. The account
of the pigs falling into the lake and drowning is "manage-
able only through a purely symbolic interpretation: the
fall of the pigs is a *figure* for the fall of rebellious spirits into
the abyss."[12] The demoniac's life among the tombs is a
symbol of alienation.[13] The verbal acrobatics are dazzling,
but they cannot conceal that the method is not really
concerned with the text, but with the "deep" (= spiritual)
meaning.

Piaget's analysis of structure, on the other hand, concentrates on the process of transformation, and rejects the
notion that there are certain fixed forms, whether of the
Platonic, Kantian, or "structuralist" variety. The three key
ideas are wholeness, transformation, and self-regulation.[14]
Wholeness means the structure in its entirety and its complex internal relationships, rather than merely an aggrega-
tion of parts.[15] Transformation involves a dialectic between the process of structuring and the result of the
process. There are no innate patterns—in language
(Chomsky) or in the human mind (Lévi-Strauss)—nor is
there "form as such" or "content as such." Rather, there
is to be discerned an ongoing process of "construction as
continual formation," whether one is dealing with senso-
ry-motor acts, operations, or theories.[16] Self-regulation
means that the transformation inherent in a structure
never leads beyond its system, but always engenders elements that belong to it and preserve its laws.[17] Illustrating
the regulatory aspect from genetics (using the theory of
C. H. Waddington), Piaget asserts that "the relation between the organism and its environment [is] a cybernetic
loop such that the organism selects its environment while
being conditioned by it."[18] In the psychological realm, the
transformation of the self is called "assimilation," which to
Piaget is "the process whereby the organism in each of its

interactions with the bodies or energies of its environment fits these in some manner to the requirements of its own physico-chemical structures while at the same time accommodating itself to them." This process of assimilation incorporates into the schema of the self objects that are familiar (recognitory assimilation) or new (generalizing assimilation). The outcome of this continual relating, setting up correspondences, and establishing functional connections is to give rise to new structures. Structure-forming characterizes the early stages of intelligence, but is an unending process in all human experience by which structures are assimilated and interstructural connections fashioned.[19]

What does the structuralist method contribute to historical study? According to Lévi-Strauss, very little. Assuming that the human mind is always and everywhere basically the same, it is the "unconscious structure underlying each institution and custom" which he claims to be exploring; or as he puts it, the superstructures (in the mind) not the infrastructures (historical phenomena).[20] Piaget objects:[21] while in social change utility alone cannot account for the formation of a structure, formation and response to contextual stimuli are interrelated. "It happens frequently that a structure changes its function to meet new social needs."[22] Finally, Piaget calls attention to the work that remains to be done on the relations between historic structures and their transformations.[23]

We have outlined in some detail the methodological issues raised by the structuralists because historians of religion, and particularly of early Christianity, have often employed the static, arbitrary methods of positivists or parallelomaniacs—to expand on a term invented by Samuel Sandmel.[24] Positivists of the left have assumed that there is nothing distinctive about Christianity, since its concepts, precepts, and rituals have parallels in other religions. Positivists of the right feel obligated to prove that there are no historical parallels to early Christianity, and that the historical uniqueness and factual accuracy of its records can be and must be demonstrated if the truth claims of Christianity are to be validated. What the structuralist approach should ask is not, "What are the parallels, if any?" but, "How have the structures inherited or constructed by early Christianity been transformed?"

## II

Speaking of the function of myths, Mol notes that they "not only interpret reality and provide a shorthand for basic personal and social experiences, but they also sacralize them. . . . They hold arbitrariness and chaos at bay, and they reinforce identity."[25] In his great work on *Myth: Its Meaning and Functions in Ancient and Other Cultures,*[26] G. S. Kirk differentiates three types of myth: (1) narrative (stories of eponymous ancestors; ethnic history); (2) operative, iterative, or validatory (related to ritual; recital to guarantee cosmic or institutional continuity; expression of faith-hopes); (3) speculative and explanatory (wrestling with fundamental problems, which seem to be divinely imposed, such as suffering and death).

Unlike the myths of creation and fall in the literature of the Hebrews and other ancient Near Eastern peoples, the Christian narrative myths recalled very recent history ("suffered under Pontius Pilate"), not primordial history ("in the beginning"). That aspect of the story of Jesus was soon incorporated into the tradition of his origins, however, as John 1:1 and Heb. 1:1–2 assert, and as Paul's suggestion of pre-existence already implies in Gal. 4:4 and Phil. 2:6. The chief mythical structure that has been adapted and transformed by the Christians to assert the transcendent role of Jesus in the creation and redemption of the world is the figure of Wisdom, who is God's agent in creating the world (Prov. 8; Wisd. Sol.; Ben Sira 24) and in revealing the divine purpose to those prepared or chosen to receive it.[27]

The more extensive construction of myth in early Christianity concerns the birth, childhood, career, death, and resurrection of Jesus. These are, of course, the themes of the Gospels. The fact that the letters of Paul and many of the so-called apocryphal gospels[28] show little or no interest in the story of Jesus, preferring rather his role as revealer-redeemer, reminds us that different structures of the life world are operative in different segments of the early church. In G. S. Kirk's terminology, Paul's myths are speculative rather than narrative. Even among the Gospels themselves, there are significant variants in the narrative mythology.

The so-called Q material stands somewhere between Paul's understanding of Jesus as heavenly revealer-redeemer and the developed narrative portrait of Jesus as human in Mark, the oldest Gospel. In the Q tradition Jesus is pictured as an eschatological prophet, whose followers will share with him in eschatological reward and vindication because they have shared with him in earthly rejection and suffering. Narrative elements are almost entirely missing, except for the extended temptation scene (Luke 4:2–12). There are links with the Wisdom tradition, but they display a transformation (of a kind already in process in postexilic Judaism)[29] of wisdom from a concept of God's providential hand in history to one of wisdom as the disclosure of God's determination of history, as it is expressed in apocalyptic literature. More is involved in this transformation than the conceptual shift: as Otto Plöger has noted,

the transition from concern for national destiny to preoc-
cupation with the future of the community of God's people "may be regarded as an act of withdrawal into a specifically religious sphere" which "bears within itself the seed
of sectarian narrowness."[30] That quality is evident in the
structure of the Qumran community, but it is also apparent in the Christian subcommunities that are behind the
Q source and the Gospel of Mark.[31]

Several features of the Gospel tradition illustrate the
dynamic interaction between continuity and change that
characterize structural transformation. The theme of the
eschatological prophet, and specifically of Elijah, is at the
same time taken over into the Jesus tradition and altered.[32] The garb of John the Baptist and the allusion to
Mal. 3:1 (in Mark 1) link him with Elijah, as does Q (Matt.
11:10; Luke 7:27) implicitly and Matthew explicitly (Matt.
11:14). Yet some think Jesus is Elijah (Mark 8:28 and par.),
while Moses (who is also an eschatological prophet in Jewish tradition)[33] and Elijah both appear in the transfiguration scene (Mark 9 and par.), where Jesus is the central
figure. The transformation of Jewish prophetic and sectarian (i.e., baptist) tradition is patent.

Similarly, the Christological titles Messiah, Son of God,
King, Son of Man are restructured and combined in new
ways in the Christian transformation of messianic structures. The range of possibilities is familiar: Messiah could
be used of the anointed priest or the anointed king; Son
of God could be a designation for the king (Psalm 2) or the
covenant people (Hos. 11) or, in a Hellenistic context, for
a divinized hero or apotheosized king; Son of Man could
refer to a human being (Ps. 8:4), to the elect remnant of
God's people (Dan. 7:13, 14, 18), or to the eschatological
agent in the parables of Enoch (if they are pre-Christian).
What is required of the historian is not the determination

as to which of the patterns fit(s) the Gospel portraits of
Jesus, but to seek to discern the process of transformation
and construction that is at work in the development of the
Christian tradition. In so doing, it is important (in Piaget's
paraphrase of Godelier) in tracing "the transition from
one structure to another" to recognize that "while the
second structure is explained in terms of this transition,
the transition itself can only be understood in transforma-
tional terms if both termini are known."[34]

Obviously not all the factors that contributed to the
early Christian transformation of structures were Jewish
in origin. The hearers and bearers of the Christian tradition included those whose life world was shaped in Greco-
Roman culture, and it is only to be expected that the
language and symbols of that culture would affect the reshaping of the tradition when Christianity moved beyond
its original sectarian Jewish environment. The narrative
myths of apocalyptic Judaism (the testing of Daniel and his
friends; the exile and wandering of the Teacher of Righteousness in the Dead Sea documents) have their counterpart in the Gospel traditions. But there are detailed features of the Hellenistic tradition of an apotheosized hero,
Heracles, which closely resemble those of the Gospels:
divine lineage, miraculous escape after birth, temptation
on the threshold of manhood, being instrumental in fulfilling the divine will on earth, inauguration of a plan of
salvation for humanity, the end of an earthly life in a
passion that is willingly accepted, the death that is wit-
nessed by the mother, is accompanied by miracles, and
leads to apotheosis.[35] When account is taken of the differences between the respective earthly careers of Jesus and
Heracles, and of the fact that many of the parallel features
are missing from the Gospel of Mark, it becomes evident
that within the range of the developing Synoptic tradition,

transformation of structures is occurring, not simply modeling of the figure of Jesus after Heracles mythology.

Similarly, the miracles of Jesus and the apostles resemble, in substance and in rhetorical style, accounts of miracles attributed to divinities; and the wonder workers who perform them function in significantly different ways, depending on the life world within which the writer (or his community) understands itself to stand. Thus, in Daniel and in the Dead Sea Scrolls, the "signs and wonders" experienced within the community are on the one hand manifestations of God's rule, and on the other hand the defeat of the God-opposing powers.[36] The wonder worker is the divinely endowed agent through whom the victory is being accomplished, in preparation for the new age. Josephus, as we have noted, reports eschatological prophets whose miracles (or promises of miracles) were supposed to be signs that they were chosen by God to prepare the Jews to survive the impending catastrophe (defeat by Rome) and enter the eschatological era.

In Hellenistic culture there were three cultural phenomena relevant to our subject which recent scholarship has often confused: miracle worker; divine wise man; aretalogy. An aretalogy is a testimony to the powers of a divinity, nearly always in connection with a healing or other act of deliverance. Aretalogies are to be found chiefly as inscriptions located at shrines of healing divinities, such as Sarapis, Isis, and Asclepius, although they also occur in literary documents, ranging from orations to scraps among the papyri.[37] Socrates is the model for the *man who is seen as divine* by reason of his wisdom, his discipline of thought and act, and his courage in the face of death.[38] D. L. Tiede notes that the image of Epicurus "as the true divine man was cultivated in Epicurean tradition in radical contrast to any image of divine presence that rested on supernatural displays of power that controverted reason." Stoics held the same view, as did Celsus.[39] Only in the third and fourth centuries, when credulity regarding miracles soared,[40] did writers like Philostratus (Life of Apollonius of Tyana) and Porphyry (Life of Pythagoras) clumsily juxtapose the miracle-working and the philosophical traditions to create a new, hybrid "divine man."[41] Philo of Alexandria, who depicts Moses as a divine man, never links that term with the working of miracles.[42]

As for the *working of miracles,* or the claim to work miracles, the attitudes ranged widely, depending on the life world from which the assessment of the claim was made. For Celsus and Lucian, "miracles" were magic or trickery or a mixture of the two. But even among those who believed in miracles, there was a range of frameworks of meaning. Theissen has written, "There is no such thing as a timeless function of miracle faith." Analysis must be carried out concerning the historical self-understanding implicit in the stories and the historical circumstances in which the stories took form. While they purport to narrate the history of Jesus, they are symbolic communications elicited by the historical Jesus:[43] in short, they are narrative myths. As such they involve more than merely conflict and integration tensions within an individual; they go beyond individual destiny to the issues of society and history. "The existential function of the texts consists in the symbolic mastery of reality."[44] The historian can learn next to nothing from the texts if he asks only or primarily, "What really happened?" However impressive the historical picture of Jesus may be, it could not of itself achieve any reconstitution of life structures and motivation in the ancient world; the form of the historical Jesus had to be elevated to the mythical Christ, with his eschatological dominance of the world and his cosmic role. Theissen has laid out a comprehensive repertoire of motifs and *dramatis personae* of the miracle stories. In this mass of material, one can instantly recognize features shared with pagan and Jewish miracle reports. The historian's task, however, is not to note superficial resemblances, but to seek to discern how the structures of the miracle stories have been transformed in the setting of the life world of the Gospel writers.[45] It is essential, however, that one analyze as precisely as possible (again, in Godelier's phrase as used by Piaget) the two termini which delimit the transformation process.

Similarly, the story of Jesus' trial and death recalls features to be found in various Jewish and pagan traditions of the period. The atoning death of the martyrs in the Maccabean period was celebrated;[46] the courage of historical figures (Socrates) and mythological characters (Heracles) in the face of death is regarded as an ideal. The death of Osiris or Dionysus and the subsequent resuscitation comprise a pattern of fertility and spiritual renewal alike. While these factors in first- and second-century culture almost certainly affected the ways in which the death of Jesus came to be interpreted by the early Christians as world-redemptive, the identification of parallels serves neither to interpret the texts adequately nor to trace the historical development of Christianity. We need to inquire after the life world in relation to which the seeming tragedy of Jesus' death came to be seen as a divine sign of deliverance. Since there was no single uniform Christian life world, and no single mythic model of redemptive death in the Jewish or wider Hellenistic cultures, the death of Jesus is mythologically depicted in a variety of ways by the early Christians.

## III

What Kirk has called operative or iterative myth[47] leads us over the bridge into ritual. Mol's definition of ritual is helpful: "the repetitive enactment of human systems of meaning." Ritual not only articulates and reiterates a system of meaning, but in so doing it also restores, reinforces, or redirects identity.[48]

As is the case with myth, structures are transformed after being taken over from or developing in parallel relation to those of other cultures. Almost certainly, baptism was the initiatory rite for the Christian movement from the outset. The model was Jesus, baptized by John on the occasion to launch his program of announcing the coming of God's rule. Whence did John derive baptism? If we say, "from Qumran," that merely moves the problem back one stage. Unlike John's baptism, which seems to have been an act of eschatological preparation by which one joined the purified people ready for the judgment, baptism in the Christian movement combined initiation with inauguration of the work of the Spirit. That interpretation is implied in the Gospel accounts of the baptism of Jesus, and is assumed throughout the Pauline corpus.[49] It serves the same function for Christians as does circumcision for Jews; at least the Pauline wing is so convinced, since Paul and his followers refuse to have circumcision as a requirement for admission to the Christian covenant community (Gal. 2–4; 5:6). For Paul, the relationship entered into in baptism was the beginning of a life of moral responsibility: "so that . . . we might walk in newness of life" (Rom. 6:4). The corporate nature of baptism is evident not only in Paul's constant references to "the body" (body of Christ = the church) into which one is baptized but also in his adaptation of the exile tradition in I Cor. 10, where the miracle of deliverance from bondage through the Red Sea is described as being "baptized into Moses in the cloud and in the sea" (I Cor. 10:2).

I Peter 3:21 utilizes a different mythological tradition—the flood—as the basis for understanding the salvific function of baptism ("saved through water"), but the writer shows the influence of Hellenistic culture by adding that the positive counterpart of the baptismal cleansing from "dirt" is the appeal to God to provide what any good Stoic would desire: "a good conscience." Hebrews 6:4 links the term "enlightened" with baptism ("those who became partakers of the Holy Spirit"). References to enlightenment are found in the magical papyri and in inscriptions related to mystery cults. Its penetration into postapostolic Christian usage is seen in the explicit reference to mystical illumination in Eph. 3:9 ("to illuminate the operation of the mystery which has been hidden in God for ages"), and it is implied in the symbolic account of Jesus' dialogue with Nicodemus ("a teacher of Israel") in John 3 ("unless one is born anew of water and the Spirit, one cannot see/enter the kingdom of God"). It becomes a commonplace in the church fathers. The changing world view—from an apocalyptic cosmos to a mystical world view—has fundamentally affected the way in which the common ritual element, baptism, is understood.

Returning to Paul's homiletical expansion of the exodus tradition in I Cor. 10, we note that he moves from water (baptism) to food and drink. The water from the rock and the manna in the desert are obvious symbols for the eucharistic wine and bread. That is explicitly stated in I Cor. 10:14-17. Not only has Paul built on the exodus mythology of ancient Israel as a way of comprehending the Communion as covenant rite, but he extrapolates from the historical experience of Israel in her disobedience to the cove-

nant as a solemn warning to the new covenant people to
avoid participation in idolatrous worship (I Cor. 10:11).

The Gospel tradition itself displays the transformation
of older tradition in interpretation of the Eucharist. That
is evident in the stories of feeding in the desert (Mark 6
and 8) where the formulaic words are used ("he took, he
blessed, he broke, he gave") even while the focus of the
miracle recalls the manna in the desert. John's version
(John 6:49–51) makes the direct comparison: "Your fathers
ate the manna in the wilderness and they died. This is the
bread which comes down from heaven, that a man may
eat of it and not die. . . . If anyone eats of this bread, he
shall live forever; and the bread which I shall give is my
flesh."[50]

Two other elements of Jewish tradition that have contributed to the development of the Eucharist are the Passover and the eschatological meal, attested at Qumran. The
Passover aspects of the Last Supper are ambiguous: the
direct statement that the meal is in celebration of the
Passover (Mark 14:12) stands in tension with the fact that
none of the essential features of the Passover celebration
is described in the narrative account of the meal (Mark
14:17–25). Other Christian traditions allude to the (pas-
chal) lamb (John 1:29; I Cor. 5:7), but there is only a vague
link with the Eucharist. The intention of the Christian use
of the Passover tradition seems to be rather general:
Christ's sacrifice makes possible the redemption of the
new covenant people, as Mark 14:24 implies.

The Eucharist as yet another mode of corporate ritual,
the eschatological meal, is suggested by the final words of
Jesus: "until that day when I drink it new in the kingdom
of God" (Mark 14:25). But it is a theme that runs through
the whole of this section of Mark: the shepherd and flock
imagery by which Jesus describes himself and his people

is tied in with apocalyptic expectation of divine vindication in Mark 14:27, where Zech. 13 is directly quoted. The
image was used earlier (Mark 6:34), just prior to the covenantal meal in the desert. A different symbol with the
same intent is used in Mark 12:1–11, where the covenant
people is portrayed as God's vineyard, a metaphor deriving from Isa. 5:1–7. It is not surprising, therefore, that the
culminating act of the ritual meal (Mark 14:25) is to share
in "the fruit of the vine" and to do so in anticipation of
eschatological deliverance. Scholars have long noted the
similarities between the Christian rite of bread and wine
and the one implied in the appendix to the Scroll of the
Rule, which is specifically stated to be a rule for the Congregation of the End Time: the blessing of the bread and
wine is carried out in the presence of the messianic priest
and the messianic king.[51] Paul's version of the eucharistic
tradition includes this element, when he remarks, "As
often as you eat this bread and drink this cup, you pro-
claim the Lord's death until he comes" (I Cor. 11:26).

Already in Paul, however, the Eucharist has taken on a
dimension of automatic efficacy that resembles magic. Indeed, Paul juxtaposes "the cup of the Lord" and "the cup
of demons" (I Cor. 10:21), with the implication that participation takes place in both instances, but that what distinguishes between them is the supernatural partner: God or
the demons. In I Cor. 11:29–30, he describes those who
have participated in the Eucharist "in an unworthy manner" and as a result have been stricken with sickness or
death. He seems to be assuming that, in addition to the
conscious intentional aspects of eucharistic participation
there are involuntary, inherent potencies at work, with
possibly sinister effects. The model for the judgment that
may fall on the covenant people corrupted by demonic
influences is the destruction of tens of thousands of Isra-

elites by serpents in the desert following their taking part in pagan worship (I Cor. 10:6–12). Jude 12, in an ambiguous metaphor, refers to those who have corrupted the sacred meals of the Christians by their carousing as either "reefs" (unseen hazards that cause shipwrecks) or "blights" that spoil the church's public and self-image.´ Their irresponsible behavior is matched by their heretical doctrine, Jude asserts (Jude 10–11). The resemblances between the Eucharist and pagan ritual meals is likewise evident in second-century Christian writings, as when Ignatius refers to "Jesus Christ's mysteries,"[52] and Justin describes how the "wicked demons" imitate the Eucharist in the mysteries of Mithras.[53] Guarantee of the validity of the Eucharist was achieved by insisting that a bishop preside or authorize someone to celebrate the Communion ritual.[54]

Yet another development of the eucharistic tradition is apparent in Luke and Acts. In the shorter and most likely original text of Luke 22:14–30, the talk concerns only the coming of the kingdom of God and the vindication following Jesus' betrayal and death. The meal appears as a ritual anticipation of the gathering of God's people in the age to come: "As my father covenanted a kingdom for me, so do I covenant for you that you may eat and drink at my table in my kingdom and sit on thrones judging the twelve tribes of Israel." The stories of the resurrection appearances of Jesus in Luke reach their climax in a ritual meal ("he took, he blessed, he broke, he gave," Luke 24:30) at which he was "known to them in the breaking of the bread" (Luke 24:35). Similarly, in Acts the disciples are represented as gathering with joy, or "with glad and generous hearts" (Acts 2:46), celebrating through "the breaking of bread" (Acts 2:42, 46; 20:7, 11; 27:35) their new role as messengers of the Gospel and their new endowment by

the Spirit of God. In Luke and Acts, references to the
memorial of Christ's death or to the sacrifice represented
by the broken body are completely absent. What is central
in the eucharistic rite is the joyous anticipation of the
eschatological fulfillment.

Although the argument from silence is weak, it is probably significant that references to the Eucharist are wholly
missing from the letter to the Hebrews. As we have noted,
there is mention of baptism, which is alluded to under the
term "enlightenment."[55] Although the author of Hebrews
treats at length of Christ's sacrifice, he does so in a framework of Platonic assumptions, in which the repeated,
ephemeral, earthly sacrifices of the Jewish cultic system
are contrasted with the once-for-all sacrifice of Christ,
which is eternal and offered in heaven. By insisting that,
by his ideal sacrifice, Christ has "abolished" the transitory
copies of the true offering (Heb. 10:9), the author suggests
there is no place in Christianity for sacrifice. Does this
include the Eucharist? One cannot be certain, but the
Eucharist is not mentioned; rather, the nearest we come
in Hebrews to ritual practice is "with our hearts sprinkled
clean from an evil conscience and our bodies washed with
pure water" (Heb. 10:22). In this passage, with its combination of Platonic ontology and Stoic ethics, the author
may be implying that there is no place for the Eucharist.
In any event, it seems not to have been a central feature
of the ritual life of his community, given the philosophical
structure in which he has interpreted the biblical tradition.

## IV

Seemingly running counter to the process of transformation of mythical structures in the early church, espe-

cially from the second century on, was the determination
to halt the adaptation of myth by consolidating it into
doctrine. The terms *didachē* and *didaskalia* are rather
rare in the Synoptic and Pauline traditions, but they are
found frequently in the post-Pauline and other second-
century writings. The revealing term regularly associated
with *didaskalia* in the pastoral letters is *hugiainein*,
which means literally to be sound and healthy, but its
derived meaning (as can be inferred from Plutarch) is to
be correct, rationally sound.[56]

A classic expression of this point of view may be found
in I Tim. 1:3–11. A technical term is employed: certain
persons are given orders not to "teach different [i.e., he-
retical] doctrine." What those now labeled heretics are
doing is occupying themselves with "myths" and specula-
tions, rather than devoting themselves to preserving the
*oikonomia* (order, economy, structure) that inheres in
faith. What "Paul" has given orders about is love, which is
characterized by "a pure heart, a good conscience, and a
faith that is free of insincerity." A lack of these qualities has
resulted in persons who seek to be Christian leaders, but
whose "vain discussion," lack of understanding, and sheer
ignorance have caused them to wander off into bad doctrine and even worse morals (vs. 9–10). The actions of the
corrupt and perverted (murderers, sodomites, kidnapers,
liars, perjurers) are seen as the direct consequence of their
perpetrators' opposition to "sound doctrine." In this literature synonyms for correct doctrine are "sound faith" or
simply "the truth" (Tit. 1:13). The true faith can be de-
viated from (I Tim. 6:10). It has been delivered to God's
holy people "once for all" (Jude 3), and is to be guarded
(II Tim. 1:12–14). It is safeguarded by the church, which
is "the pillar and bulwark of the truth" (I Tim. 3:15). In
summarizing its doctrine, "Paul" cries out (using a phrase

which is never found in his authentic letters, but which is
a commonplace term of Hellenistic piety): "Great indeed,
we confess, is the mystery of our religion" (I Tim. 3:16).

What has happened is far more than the transformation
of mythical or ritual structures as such. The social structure of the church is itself in process of transformation, and
its "sacred cosmos" is being radically overhauled—at least
by the wing of early Christianity represented by Ephesians, the pastoral letters, and Jude. Faith is for them right
doctrine. Moral responsibility is dependent on conscience.
The church must be concerned about its public image (I
Tim. 3:1–7). Piety is on a do-it-yourself basis (I Tim. 4:7).
Special instructions are offered to the rich in the church
(I Tim. 6:17). In short, the community behind these documents is the early-second-century equivalent of a middle-
to-upper-middle-class organization, worried about its reputation, the tightness of its hierarchy, the purity of its
doctrine, and the stability of its enterprise throughout suc-
ceeding generations (II Tim. 1:5). It still speaks of "that
Day" (II Tim. 1:12) and of Jesus' "appearing" (though it
uses the general Hellenistic term for mystical disclosure,
*epiphaneia,* rather than the eschatological term *parousia;*
see II Tim. 1:10). But immortality has already been revealed and death has already been "abolished." The fervor and expectancy of the earlier eschatological community has been replaced by a bourgeois group that still
speaks of persecution (II Tim. 1:16; 4:6), but seems chiefly
concerned about doctrinal unity (Eph. 4:5, 13) and pious
respectability (II Tim. 3:5).[57]

V

Diversities among the New Testament writers are likewise apparent in attitudes toward the state, and therefore

in the positions adopted on *political* issues. The very existence of Christianity, to say nothing of its varied fortunes
in relation to Rome, was directly affected by the different
stances assumed by the movement toward the political
structures and powers.

The apocalyptic view of history evident in Mark stood
in the tradition of Daniel and Qumran on the political
issues:[58] the position was one of noninvolvement, in view
of the expectation that all worldly powers were soon to be
brought to an end by direct divine action. Meanwhile,
minimum obligations to the state were to be discharged,
as attested by the familiar word of Jesus, "Render to Caesar . . ." (Mark 12:17 and par.).

Here Jesus appears to be taking a point of view similar
to that of Paul (Rom. 13), which also resembles that of the
Pharisees. Paul seems to have taken this position, as did
Jesus, in confidence that the relatively tolerant attitude of
Rome toward local religious movements provided the opportunity for the work of the Gospel to be carried out
unhindered. The mission could be fulfilled only if political
and civil order were maintained throughout the empire.

Ironically, both Jesus and Paul were executed as threats
to the *pax Romana.* While we know nothing—other than
later legend—about the circumstances of Paul's death, it
may be inferred that he died as an alleged subverter of the
state religion, on the observance of which both the good-
will of the gods and the loyalty of the empire's subjects
were believed to depend.

In the Gospel accounts of the execution of Jesus, the
factors are more complex. The one overwhelmingly certain historical fact is that Jesus was put to death by the
Roman authorities on the charge of insurrection, as both
the mode of execution and the public notice, "King of the
Jews" (Mark 15:26), confirm.[59] It is most unlikely that an

apolitical Markan community would have invented such a
politically freighted phrase. Since Jesus is reported to have
used the rhetoric of monarchy from the onset of his ministry (Mark 1:15) and since the nationalist aspirations were
linked with him in the form of the messianic (Mark 8:29)
and dynastic (Mark 10:47; 12:35) titles his followers reportedly used, it is not at all surprising that he appeared to the
civil authorities to be a pretender to political power.

The question[60] has been raised since at least the eigh-
teenth century[60] as to whether the accusation of sedition
against Jesus was true. Early in this century that theory
was revived by a Marxist historian, Karl Kautsky, who
wanted to portray Jesus as the persecuted founder of a
proletarian liberation movement,[61] a position that was developed and for which documentation was adduced by
Robert Eisler, and more recently by S. G. F. Brandon in
his *Jesus and the Zealots.*[62] The issue has been raised and
analyzed by Martin Hengel, both as a historical problem
and as a response to contemporary revolutionaries who
want to portray their heroes as modern counterparts of
Jesus, the alleged organizer of a popular revolt.[63] After
showing that Josephus has intentionally played down this
aspect of Palestinian Judaism, Hengel concludes that Zealots (whom the Romans called *sicarii,* and to whom Josephus gives the innocuous designation *lēstai* (bandits), carried on guerrilla warfare against the Romans throughout
the first century, down to the organization of full-scale
revolt in A.D. 66. As Hengel shows, Jesus' entry into Jerusalem and his actions in the Temple were affairs of small
dimension, with symbolic significance for the early
church, but with no implications of insurrection so far as
the Romans were concerned. Had the latter been evident,
the Roman troops would have rushed down from their
guard posts in the Tower of Antonia and halted his activi-

ties. The swords mentioned as part of the equipment of
the disciples (Luke 22:35–38) were for personal protection
on their travels, not for armed revolt. Invitations to exercise political force were rejected by Jesus, according to the
Gospel tradition. While he was critical of exploitive
wealth, he befriended the tax collectors and aided minor
Roman authorities. He is pictured, not as a disciplined,
ascetic organizer, but as "a glutton and a drunkard," who
recommends and emulates the life-style of the birds and
the wild flowers. His mission is to heal wounds, not to
inflict them; to love his enemies, both in attitude and action (Luke 6:27–29), not to kill them.[64] Hengel offers this
sound historical observation: "In the ensuing forty years
until the Neronian persecution, the Roman government
took no more action against the Christians in Palestine.
. . . The crucifixion of the messianic pretender, Jesus, had
closed the case so far as Pilate was concerned."[65]

One could imagine that, with the waning of expectation
of eschatological fulfillment, the church might have
turned to direct political action (as had one wing of the
Hasidim).[66] But the response took other directions in the
restructuring of eschatological mythology. An important
segment of the church retained the rhetoric but concentrated on unification and organization of doctrine and
practice (Ephesians and the pastoral epistles). Another
group preserved the contrast between this age and the
age to come by projecting their hopes into the heavenly
realm of eternal realities (Hebrews). Yet another community turned inward, perceiving its hopes to be fulfilled
through the timeless mystical communion between the
Vine and the branches, between the Shepherd and the
sheep (John): "The hour is coming and now is . . ."

Two documents within the New Testament address the
issue of church and state more nearly overtly, but do so in

sharply different ways. One is The Revelation to John, which follows the lead of Daniel in denouncing the idolatrous civil authorities, but does so in cryptic form and in symbolism, the import of which would be known only by the esoteric group for whom the document was produced. John of the Revelation expects martyrdom for many of his fellow Christians. Probably he was writing during the reign of Domitian (81–96),[67] when persecution of Christians began again. John the Seer's community clearly regards itself as an elect minority, determined to resist the demands of an idolatrous state, but with no inclination to take up arms, even in self-defense, by way of resistance or revolt.

The other document that treats of conflicts on the sociopolitical level is Luke-Acts, although it handles the issue in a rather subtle and low-pressure fashion. Repeatedly the author goes out of his way (as comparison with Synoptic parallels will show) to introduce references to political powers before whom the events of the founding of Christianity transpired. From the synchronism that introduces the public ministry of John the Baptist (Luke 3:1–3), through the mention of the special hearing before Herod Antipas (Luke 23:6–12), Luke conveys to his reader the clear impression that Christianity is an event open to the public, taking place under official scrutiny. In Acts the same feature is evident, but with the added implication that the civil authorities in no case found Christians guilty of violating Roman law or threatening the stability of the state (Acts 16:39; 18:14–16; 19:37; 23:29; 25:8, 25; 26:32). The author's implicit defense of Christians is placed on the lips of Paul: "Is it lawful for you to scourge a man who is a Roman citizen and uncondemned?" (Acts 22:25). The accusation made against Paul by "a certain Tertullus" in a hearing before Felix, the Roman governor, may not be

an actual report, but it seems to represent accurately what
the Christians were encountering (Acts 24:1ff.). Paul is
described as "an agitator among all the Jews throughout
the world, and a ringleader of the sect of the Nazarenes."
Although their morality and monotheism were widely ad-
mired, the Jews were regarded as nonconformists—and
therefore as subversives in the Roman empire—because of
their refusal to participate in the imperial cult. Christians
shared the same opprobrium, but compounding the hostility toward them was the widespread charge that they
performed secret rites, obscene or cannibalistic (a dis-
torted report of the Eucharist, no doubt). It is to combat
charges of this sort that Paul reportedly affirms, "Neither
against the law of the Jews, nor against the temple, nor
against Caesar have I offended" (Acts 25:8). Neither is
there anything secret about the events of which Paul and
his colleagues preach, because "this thing has not happened hidden away in a corner" (Acts 26:26, TEV). Christianity is a public phenomenon and can survive full public,
judicial scrutiny. It is neither esoteric nor subversive. In
spite of tensions with political authorities, Christianity is a
law-abiding nonpolitical movement, according to Luke-
Acts.

In the second and third centuries Christianity gained
high visibility, while retaining its stance against the imperial cult at the very time when divine honors to the emperor were being promoted as a device to bind together
a fragmented empire. Intellectuals, motivated by philosophical disdain and scorn of what they regarded as irra-
tionality, joined with the imperial powers to try to stamp
out Christianity. The thoughtful opposition of Marcus
Aurelius (161–180), the persecution under Decius (249–
251), and the scorn of Lucian and Celsus could not offset
the appeal of Christianity, however. The piety of its adher-

ents at their best, the intellectual skill of its apologists and scholars, the inclusiveness of its community across social and ethnic barriers, and its claim to true ecumenicity enabled it to stand in the face of imperial hostility. But though it withstood the opposition, it was profoundly transformed in the process, with respect to its myth, its ritual, and its changing world views, and therefore with respect to the sense of personal and social identity that it provided. It is in the literature produced in the early stages of this process—documents that we know as the New Testament—that the range of structural and strategic options and the details of the transformation are most apparent. And it is to the social dimensions of that literature that we now address our attention.

# 6

# SOCIAL FUNCTIONS OF THE NEW TESTAMENT WRITINGS

In their classic study, *Theory of Literature*,[1] René Wellek and Austin Warren discuss both "extrinsic" and "intrinsic" approaches to literature. The former deal with the relation of literature to biography, psychology, society, and the history of ideas; the latter treat style, meter, genre, and other literary features and modes. Here our concern is primarily with the extrinsic aspects of New Testament literature, and it may be well to observe some of the cautions noted by Wellek and Warren.

The first warning is against limiting the criticism of a literary work to an assessment of the author's intention in writing it: "The total meaning of a work cannot be defined merely in terms of its meaning for the author and his contemporaries."[2] The work "leads an independent life" and must be assessed in the light of its impact at various junctures in the history of its interpretation and criticism. It is legitimate to attempt "to interpret literature in the light of its social context and antecedents," but it is illegitimate when the interpretation "becomes a 'causal' explanation, professing to account for literature, to explain it, and finally to reduce it to its origins."[3] Wellek and Warren settle for a modest expectation: they "seek to establish only some degree of relationship between the work of art

126

and its setting," and they "assume that some degree of illumination follows from such knowledge."[4]

What are some of the aspects of literature that may be illuminated through analysis of social context? First, it must be acknowledged that language, symbolism, and certain literary conventions are social in their very nature. The author is a member of a society and writes for a readership. Worth investigating are the social status of the writer, the degree of his or her dependence for social and economic support, although the social origins of a writer may be different from the social setting of the work, given a writer's potential for upward mobility.[5] Nevertheless, important clues about a work are the linguistic and literary features which it embodies, as indicators of the general cultural climate in which it was produced.[6] Wellek and Warren note that a literary work can be used as a social document and thereby "yield the outlines of social history." Furthermore, the sociology-of-knowledge approach has an advantage over other sociological approaches—that of exposing the presuppositions and implications of the position adopted by the writer (as well as by the investigator).[7] On the other hand, in addition to finding the method "excessively historicist," they consider it unable to provide a rational foundation for aesthetics and hence for criticism and evaluation.[8] Although these caveats serve to warn against assuming that attention to the social and cultural context of a work of literature will furnish some sort of final, comprehensive explanation of a document, two aspects of the aims of Wellek and Warren are so different from our aims as to qualify their warnings: (1) their ultimate interest is in aesthetic evaluation, which is no real concern of ours; and (2) they acknowledge the value of sociological analysis for determining "the possibility of realization of certain aesthetic values, but not the values themselves."[9]

With this we may agree, but with qualifications. If we modify that quest for values to include bringing into focus the range of social values and institutions, aspirations, and fears represented in the various segments of Greco-Roman society, then we shall be in a better position to recognize features that early Christianity shared with contemporary culture and also to place in bold relief those distinctive features which contrast sharply with the movement's social context.

In their discussion of the "intrinsic study of literature," Wellek and Warren advocate what they call "perspectivism," by which they mean "a process of getting to know the object from different points of view which may be defined and criticized in their turn."[10] When the data base is as narrow as it is in the historical study of Christian origins—twenty-seven short books, most of which are anonymous, or pseudonymous and of unknown provenance—an important and relatively underutilized angle of perspective *is* the analysis of social factors, as implicit in these documents and as known from sources contemporary with the rise of Christianity. While "some degree of illumination" of a text achieved by establishing "some degree of relationship between [a New Testament writing] and its setting" may sound insufficient for the aesthetically oriented literary critic, it constitutes what Ricoeur calls "traces" (see Chapter 1) and as such can be a priceless asset for the historian.

One of the intrinsic aspects of literature scrutinized by Wellek and Warren is *genre*. Describing genre as a "literary institution," they quote Harry Levin: "One can work through, express himself through existing institutions, create new ones, or get on, as far as possible without sharing in polities or rituals; one can also join, but then reshape institutions."[11] Two observations they make in connection with this concept of genre as institution are especially relevant for us. First, the genres shift. They represent a repertoire of possibilities "available to the writer and already intelligible to the reader. The good writer partly conforms to the genre as it exists, partly stretches it." The second observation is more subjective: "By and large, great writers are not inventors of genres."[12]

The range of possibilities suggested here for modification of a genre calls to mind the process of transformation of structures sketched in our discussion of cult and culture (Chapter 5). Here we are told that genres invite reshaping to serve new purposes; there we were reminded that old structures can be used to serve new ends. Both observations are important for our exploration of the New Testament from the perspective of sociology of literature. It is by no means sufficient to ask, What generic kinship is there between the New Testament writings and other works of the same epoch? The question is rather, How did the early Christians transform the literary structures of their time to serve new objectives within their community?

I

The oldest Christian literary tradition is that of the letters of Paul.[13] Probably the preserved letters (I and II Thessalonians, Galatians, Romans, I and II Corinthians, Philippians, Philemon, and probably Colossians) represent communications from Paul to the churches only during the latter half of his ministry (i.e., after A.D. 50). But Paul's practice of keeping in touch by letter with the churches under his charge seems to have been standard with him before that time (cf. II Thess. 3:17). He mentions other letters that have not been preserved (I Cor. 5:9; II Cor. 2:4; Col. 4:16). So fixed was Paul's mode of communication by letter and so authoritative the import of his letters that they were exchanged among churches (Col. 4:16), and letters purporting to be by Paul appeared in the church after his death (Ephesians; I and II Timothy; Titus). What precedent was there for letters as formal means of communication in the Greco-Roman period? And what social function did they serve in the Pauline churches?

Writings in the form of letters have been preserved in large numbers from Hellenistic and Roman culture. They range in quality from the literarily self-conscious epistolary form used by Seneca and Epicurus; through the official correspondence between a provincial governor (Pliny the Younger) and the emperor (Trajan); to the purely personal communications found in the papyri, chiefly from Egypt. Already in this epistolary spectrum can be perceived a wide range of social functions. Yet the letters of the New Testament do not fit neatly into any of these descriptive categories.

The basic format of a letter of the period is clear: identification of the sender and the recipient, with some pious greeting; the invocation of a deity, with thanks; the body of the letter; closing benedictions and petitions with greetings; a closing note written by the sender himself. Many simple letters of this sort have been recovered. They include, for example, an account of a tourist's journey on the Nile, a message from a homesick runaway to his father, and the somewhat self-satisfied report of a new military recruit. The letters often include "thanks to our Lord Sarapis" and stylized declarations of good wishes for the welfare of friends.[14] The Hellenistic pattern was somewhat modified in Jewish usage, as the Letter of Aristeas attests.[15]

Paul, however, felt free to modify the conventions of his

time, both in detail and in substance. For example, instead of greeting the recipients with the stylized *chairete* of pagan usage, Paul employs a kind of pun, *charis,* to which he adds the Greek equivalent of the traditional Jewish *shalom* to create his own distinctive greeting, "grace and peace." Beyond the formula, he inserts in the midst of this prescript statements concerning his gospel and his apostolic office (cf. Rom. 1:1–7; Gal. 1:1–3). Similarly, the greetings extended to individuals in the churches far exceed what we should expect on the analogy of personal letters in the papyri. Paul's reasons for adapting the epistolary style of his era are significant for understanding his letters.

First, Paul employs the letter as an instrument of his own apostolic authority. He cannot be in all his churches at once, but his spirit can be and, in his view, *is* there (I Cor. 5:4). His spirit is at work "with the power of our Lord Jesus" in the solemn judicial act of excommunication (5:5). In the next paragraph of the same letter, Paul refers twice to what he has written to the Corinthian Christians, and does so in order to reinforce his official instructions, not merely to refresh their memories. What he said in his earlier letter (5:9) is strengthened in this letter, "but now I write . . ." (5:11). Analogously, their inquiries to him on the subject of marriage (7:1) have an official dimension, requiring a formal response, which is embodied in this letter. Yet it is not only in rebuke but also in tender admonition that his apostolic function is evident: "I do not write this to make you ashamed, but to admonish you as my beloved children" (4:14). He goes on to describe himself as their "father." The letter is for Paul the means by which both the affective[16] and authoritative dimensions of his apostolic office are discharged toward the community under his responsibility. There is exact correspondence between his apostolic presence in the flesh and in his letters (II Cor. 10:10–11).

A second closely related function of the letter for Paul is as a mode of instruction. In this respect, Paul's letters more nearly resemble literary epistles, such as Seneca's, in which the aim is not mutual communication but pedagogy. As for the authority behind his teaching, Paul combines two sources: his commissioning by Christ and his collegial relationship with the other apostles. Thus the conflict with Peter detailed in Galatians is to be resolved on the basis of Paul's having been "set apart" for the Gentile mission (Gal. 1:16), and the confirmation of that mission by the assembled apostles in Jerusalem (Gal. 1:23; 2:7–10). The combined factors of divine revelation and a stance within the apostolic tradition are evident in Paul's instructions concerning the Eucharist (I Cor. 11:23) and the gospel which he preaches (I Cor. 15:3–11). He can on occasion stress the special nature of his own mystical experience, when he was taken up into the presence of God (II Cor. 12:1–7), an experience which he claims happened frequently (II Cor. 12:7, "the abundance of revelations"). But he mentions this only to reassure the Corinthians that he possesses the same spiritual gifts as do the other apostles (II Cor. 12:11), and that the same miraculous powers were evident through him as were claimed by the other apostles and their champions. The divine source of his instruction receives confirmation through its conformity to the human pattern of the other apostles.

Romans is unique among the letters of Paul in that it was certainly written to a church that he had not founded, (although if Paul wrote Colossians, that letter could be similarly classified). He seeks to establish his credentials in Rome by means of this letter, in which are employed both existential and intellectual devices. Paul concludes the letter with the fullest account of his own travels and plans to be found in any of his surviving writings, and then appends by far the longest list of persons to whom he extends greetings. Since Rome is a place he had not yet visited (Rom. 1:10) and where he does not intend to remain (Rom. 15:24), the only plausible explanation for the extensive personal greetings is that he wanted to establish rapport with the Christians there and to gain their acceptance. On the intellectual side, he wrote to them a letter which, though it included these personal elements, is the only surviving systematic statement of his understanding of the covenant community: how it stands in the overall purpose of God, and how persons can become and remain part of that community. Paul wanted to demonstrate by means of a letter the potential universality of the Christian community and of his own apostolic role. The "obedience of faith" through Paul's apostleship was to be "among all the nations" (Rom. 1:5). What is in essence a personal letter from Paul to a group of Christians in Rome is the instrument for setting forth that claim. The Hellenistic literary structure known as the letter or epistle has been transformed by the Christian community to serve its own distinctive ends.

## II

At the same time that Paul was consolidating his churches and his apostolic role by means of letters, Christians in Palestine and Syria were being nurtured by and were transmitting (as well as producing?) oral tradition about Jesus. Like Paul, the bearers of this Jesus tradition appealed to encounter with and commissioning by Jesus as the ground of their authority (Mark 6; Matt. 10; Luke 9). Like Paul's apostolic role, their assignments were confirmed by heavenly visions (Mark 9) and by postresur-

rection appearances (Matt. 28; Luke 24). Apart from the
eucharistic words in I Cor. 11, Paul makes only passing
reference to what Jesus said. For example, there is perhaps
an allusion in I Cor. 7:10 to the saying of Jesus about divorce and remarriage in Mark 10:2–9. Other traditions of
sayings of Jesus, apart from the Gospels, were preserved
in certain segments of the early church, as attested by Acts
20:35 ("remembering the words of the Lord Jesus . . ."").
The formula that introduces those words is found in Acts
11:16, as well as in I Clement (13:1; 46:7) and Letter of
Polycarp (2:3). The collections of sayings of Jesus found in
the Coptic Gnostic library at Nag Hammadi, including the
Gospel of Thomas and the Gospel of Truth, show that this
sayings tradition continued to be used and to grow long
after the canonical Gospels were completed.

There is one source, however, which seems to represent
a kind of meeting ground between the oral and the written forms of the Jesus tradition, and which offers the best
clues as to how that material functioned in the segment of
primitive Christianity that preserved it. Although the debate continues over the question as to whether there was
a common source drawn upon by Matthew and Luke[17]—
the so-called Q source—the strong probability is that there
was such a collection and that it was preserved in written
form. As E. Güttgemanns has pointed out in his study of
form criticism, the phenomenon of oral literature must be
understood strictly on the basis of the creative process of
each new performance. There is a fundamental gap between oral and written literature; to speak of a normative
form of oral tradition is to describe a phantom. When,
however, oral material is reduced to writing, we have a
third category, different from either of the other two.[18] If
we assume that the Q material, which is almost entirely
sayings rather than narrative in nature, circulated origi-

nally in oral form, what does that imply about the community that preserved it?

The whole of the Q tradition is eschatologically oriented, including the story of the centurion's servant (Luke 7:2–3, 6–10), which serves as a model for the inclusion of faithful Gentiles in the community of faith. Referring to Luke for our examples, the themes under which the Q material may be grouped appropriately are as follows:

Discipleship: Its Privileges and Trials
   Luke 6:20–49; 9:57–62; 10:2–20; 10:21–23; 11:2–13; 12:51–53; 14:16–24; 14:26–27; 16:13; 17:3–6
The Prophet as God's Messenger
   Luke 3:7–9, 16–17; 11:49–51; 12:2–3; 12:4–10, 11–12, 42–46; 13:34–35; 16:16–17
Repentance or Judgment
   Luke 11:33–36; 11:39–48, 52; 12:54–59; 13:14–29; 17:23–30, 35, 37; 19:12–13, 15–26
Jesus as Revealer and Agent of God's Rule
   Luke 4:2b–12; 7:18–35; 10:24; 11:14–22; 13:20–21; 15:4–7; 22:28–30

The figure of Jesus as presented in the Q material is a prime example of the charismatic leader discussed in Chapter 3 above, and especially the eschatological prophet. Prepared for his role by baptism and through his successful contest with Satan, Jesus is portrayed in the Q source as one whose moral pronouncements are made in the light of the coming of God's rule, and whose mighty works are both a sign of the overcoming of the powers of evil and a summons to repentance. The family is redefined in terms of those who are truly followers of Jesus, who hate their earthly families, who have abandoned all the ordinary securities of house and job in order to join with him in announcing the coming of God's kingdom. The disciples are sent out to extend the ministry of Jesus, in healing and exorcisms, as well as in the pronouncement of judgment on the impenitent. Insight as to who Jesus is and what God is even now accomplishing through him is vouchsafed to the inner circle of his followers.

Many of the statements—especially predictions—attributed to Jesus in the Q source are stylized in form. Some exhibit the pattern, "as it was . . . so shall it be"; others are distinguishable by the introductory words, "if anyone . . ." or "whoever does . . ."[19] They are attributed to Jesus, but may well come, at least in part, from Christian prophets in the early church. From the standpoint of Q, that makes no difference, since the work of the disciples in this interim before the fulfillment of the eschatological hope is an extension of the work begun by Jesus, is carried on by his authority, and is authorized by the commission the disciples received from him. They will share the rule with him in the age to come, and will be vindicated then. The very fluidity of the borderline between what may have come from Jesus and what is uttered in his name by his disciples supports the notion that oral tradition—even oral tradition that has been recorded—is of a different order than written tradition. The way in which members of the community that preserved this tradition—or helped, by prophetic oracles, to produce it—is accurately reflected in Luke 10:21–22 (=Matt. 11:25–27):

> I thank thee, Father, Lord of heaven and earth, that thou hast hidden these things from the wise and understanding and revealed them to babes; yea, Father, for such was thy gracious will. All things have been delivered to me by my Father; and no one knows who the Son is except the Father, or who the Father is except the Son and any one to whom the Son chooses to reveal him.

The prophetic, revelatory role of the founder of the community is explicit here, as is the conventicle character of the esoteric group that stands behind Q and rejoices in its hidden knowledge of the divine purpose. There is in the Q tradition no story of the passion, although the suffering of the faithful and the rejection of God's final message in Jerusalem are described. There is explicit reference to taking up the cross (Luke 14:27). Persevering in the trials with Jesus is seen as an essential prerequisite to sharing in the life of the people of the new covenant (Luke 22: 28–30). The contrast between the alienation and marginality experienced by the disciples "now" and the eschatological vindication, is vividly expressed in the beatitudes of Q (in Luke's version):

Blessed are you poor, for yours is the kingdom of God.
Blessed are you that hunger now, for you shall be satisfied.
Blessed are you that weep now, for you shall laugh.

The reversal of fortunes in the impending new age is a central theme of the community behind Q. Their vindication is imminent and certain.[20]

In Mark, many of the same features are evident: the sense of alienation, the conviction that the disciples' ministry of preaching and healing and exorcisms is an extension of Jesus' work for the kingdom of God, the expectation of suffering, and the confidence in an early vindication by divine intervention. What is different from Q, however, is that the community has developed rules for guiding its own internal corporate life in the interim before the eschaton. The authority for those rules is, of course, to be found in the words of Jesus. But the issues dealt with are not primarily eschatological: divorce and remarriage, attitudes toward the state and toward wealth. Theological issues are also treated, such as the resurrection, the First

Commandment, the messianic question about Son of David, Sabbath observance, the forgiveness of sins. All are set in the context of controversy with Jewish interpreters of the Scriptures. This context may go back to the life situation of Jesus, but it certainly reflects the setting in which the Markan community is living and carrying out its mission. The combination within Mark of ethical instruction, apocalyptic prediction, and narrative depicting the circumstances leading up to the founding of the community—including Jesus' call and baptism, temptation, commissioning of his followers, growing official hostility, trial, and death—recalls the Dead Sea Scrolls, and especially the Damascus Document and the Scroll of the Rule. What we have in Mark is the foundation document of an apocalyptic Christian sect. Although there are only bits of evidence by which to hypothesize the provenance of Mark, there is a convergence of factors that point to rural and small-town southern Syria: the mode of house-building and of farming, as well as the place names mentioned, point to this area; the document was written in crude but fluent Greek (employing the LXX for quotations), yet with traces of Semitic usage behind the Greek. The refusal of the Markan community to side with either the nationalists or the assimilationists in the war with Rome also makes historical sense in that area, on the basis of Josephus' reports of intra-Jewish conflicts there in the 60's.[21]

Unlike the Qumran community, which withdrew to the desert in order to maintain ritual purity, the Markan group was both inclusive and evangelistic. Nevertheless, its sectarian quality is evident in the claim to have secret knowledge (Mark 4:11); to have received private visions followed by private explanations (9:2–9); and to possess the clues to understanding cryptic documents (13:14). The community's hopes are to be fulfilled within the lifetime of their own generation (13:30). Their sacrifice in abandoning houses, families, and lands is soon to be compensated for "in the age to come" (10:30). One can perceive behind this Gospel a community bound together by zeal, commitment, and expectation. There is no evidence of structure or of chain of command. All the ordinary socioeconomic structures have been abandoned in the service of the proclamation of God's rule. Founded by itinerant charismatics,[22] these conventicles had no basis for survival after the expectation was disappointed,[23] or for ongoing organization, or for cooperating with other and more sociologically stable segments of early Christianity. The chief contribution of the Markan group was the creation of a new genre, the Gospel. Since the Gospel served a specific function in the esoteric, eschatologically oriented group that produced it, there should be no surprise that the structure of the Gospel was significantly altered as it was adapted to other functions by other Christian groups with a different life world than the Markan outlook.

The only other writing within the New Testament dominated by the apocalyptic outlook is, of course, the book of Revelation. In literary terms, it combines with the apocalypse proper (Rev. 4–22) a series of letters (Rev. 2–3), although the letters are themselves communications in the spirit and style—and with the world view—of an apocalypticist. The emphasis falls on the incorrigibility of the evil forces apart from a divine catastrophic intervention in history. There are warnings to those who might waver and encouragements to those who persist, even to the point of martyrdom. The imagery is familiar in general from Daniel and other apocalypses, but the writer has reworked and expanded the material into some of the most vivid imagery and literarily most effective passages in all of early Christian literature. The specific historical

setting out of which the book comes is suggested by the
place names mentioned—all from Asia Minor—and the
central issue of the imperial cult point to the reign of
Domitian (A.D. 81–96). From Suetonius' *Life of Domitian*
we know that he demanded recognition as *Dominus et
Deus,* which Christians could only regard as idolatrous and
impossible for them. Efforts to determine the identity of
the emperor in question on the basis of deciphering the
images of Rev. 13 and 17, with their "heads" and "beasts,"
are inconclusive, but these images are not inappropriate
for Domitian. Presumably I Peter points to the same crisis
at the same time. In both documents, the Christians' refusal to participate in the imperial cult is regarded by the
authorities as a subversive act, for which the punishment
was execution. While in Mark 13 the threat to Christians
is from Jewish authorities and petty local rulers, in Revelation it is the imperial power itself which must be con-
fronted and resisted to the death. Clearly, by the reign of
Domitian the Christian movement has become a public
phenomenon, even though something of the sectarian
spirit holds the group firm in the face of persecution and
death. In Mark the final visitation of judgment that will
precede the end of the age is the destruction of the Temple in Jerusalem; in Revelation, it is the fall of Rome itself
(Rev. 18).

The Gospel of Matthew exemplifies the transformation
of structures within the Christian movement itself. The
core of Matthew resembles and incorporates the Gospel of
Mark. But the beginning and the end, as well as substantial
additions and modifications within the section dealing
with the career of Jesus, represent substantive alteration
of form and function, not simple supplementation. Although Mark has built his narrative throughout, but especially in the passion narrative,[24] on the basis of fulfillment

of Scripture, Matthew has made this an explicit, dominant factor throughout his Gospel. It is evident in the opening genealogies, which trace the lineage of Jesus back to Abraham and David, placing the Gospel story in continuity with the history of Israel. Each stage in the infancy stories is in fulfillment of Scripture (Matt. 1:22; 2:5, 15, 17; 2:23), as is the coming of John the Baptist (with Mark's mingled quotation from Malachi and Isaiah corrected) in Matt. 3:3. Each of the temptations of Jesus is met with a quotation from Scripture, and Scripture is cited to explain his residence in Galilee (Matt. 4:15–16).

Although the pattern is not carried out consistently, the expression, "When Jesus had finished . . ."—which is repeated five times (Matt. 7:28; 11:1; 13:53; 19:1; 26:1)— seems to have been intended to mark off a fivefold structure to the book. Each section consists of a narrative followed by a discourse. The discourses are The Sermon on the Mount (Matt. 5–7), The Messianic Mission (Matt. 9:36 to 10:42), The Parables of the Kingdom (Matt. 13), Accountability Within the Community (Matt. 18), Matthew's Version of the Apocalypse (greatly expanded from Mark) in Matt. 24. Almost certainly,[25] Matthew has structured his book in conscious imitation of the five books of Moses, an inference which receives support in the opening discourse from the setting over against each other of the authority of Jesus and that of Moses: "You have heard that it has been said [i.e., by Moses] . . . but I say to you . . ." That issue comes to a head in the long, distinctively Matthean passage (Matt. 23:1–36) which makes contact at points with Markan and Q material, but which is unique in setting Pharisaic interpretation of the law over against that of Jesus, and which is without parallel in the New Testament for its vindictive, vengeful denunciation of the Jews: "That upon you may come all the righteous blood shed on

earth . . ." (Matt. 23:35). The murders mentioned (Abel
and Zechariah) are the first and last to be described in the
Bible, so that the whole weight of the death of the innocent is placed upon the Jews; and Matthew adds, "Truly,
I say to you, all this will come *upon this generation"* (Matt.
23:36). Clearly, the community behind Matthew stands in
bitterest conflict and competition with Pharisaic Judaism.
It shares with them the belief in "the law and the prophets" (Matt. 5:17) and in the certainty of their fulfillment.
Where it disagrees violently is that the agent rejected by
the Jewish authorities and by those who share their views
is indeed the one chosen by God to bring about the fulfillment of this hope and this heritage.

Matthew's attitude toward the law and the moral obligations contained in it are far removed from those of Paul.
The law is not to be relaxed among Christians, but the
righteousness of the members of this community is to exceed in stringency that of the scribes and Pharisees (Matt.
5:19–20). The single area in which literal conformity to the
law is not required is the matter of food and ritual cleanli-
ness: what one does and thinks ("out of the heart") is the
source of evil, not what one touches or eats (Matt. 15:11,
19–20).

In the initial stages, at least, the mission of the disciples
is to be limited to Israel (Matt. 10:5). The "lost sheep" who
are expected to respond to the gospel probably are the
faithful remnant to be delivered by the shepherd-king
according to the oracles of Zechariah (Zech. 9–11; 13). The
identification of Jesus with this figure is explicit in Matt.
21:5 (= Zech. 9:9), and the link between Jesus' impending
death and the smitten shepherd (Zech. 13:7) is taken over
by Matthew from Mark at the point in the passion story
where the disciples are about to flee. Thus, for Matthew's
community, the church is the true Israel,[26] the true heir

to the promises, and the fulfillment of her aspirations. Yet this understanding of the covenant community is not merely a reversion to an earlier point of view; rather, the potential members of the covenant people are from "all nations" (Matt. 28:19). For them, the teachings of Jesus—"all that I have commanded you"—have replaced the law of Moses as the authoritative norm for the life of the new covenant people. The end of the age is still expected (Matt. 28:20), but, in contrast to Mark 16:7, it is not a time of initial reunion: "Lo, I am with you always, to the close of the age" (Matt. 28:20). The standards are set forth for the ongoing community, including even judicial procedures for settling disputes (Matt. 18:15–20). The church of Matthew, with the apostolic foundation going back to Peter as sovereign and arbiter (Matt. 16:16–18), is an established institution, not an apocalyptic sect.

## III

Two features strike the reader of Luke and Acts: one is the very fact that the story of Jesus moves without interruption into the story of the spread of Christianity from the center of the Jewish world to its arrival in the Gentile world capital, Rome; the other is the literarily pretentious way in which each of these two books begins (Luke 1:1–4; Acts 1:1–5), including even an address to the author's patron, Theophilus. The life world of the author, and presumably of the community which he is addressing, involves a sharply different stance toward Greco-Roman culture than that represented in Mark or Matthew. And the attitude toward both this age and the age to come diverges in important ways from that of Mark or Q, and probably Matthew. Language, rhetoric, and literary forms all show the positive influence of Hellenistic models. The search for God on the part of pagan poets and philosophers is regarded as commendable, even though inadequate (Acts 17). The absence and seeming delay of Christ is not regarded as a problem, since God is portrayed as actively present now through his Spirit (Luke 24; Acts 1). The coming of Christ is regarded as certain, but not imminent (Acts 1:8–11).

The worldwide mission of the church is not merely mentioned, as in Matt. 28:19, but is prepared for paradigmatically by the outpouring of the Spirit on "devout men from every nation under heaven" at Pentecost (Acts 2:5), launched through the work of the apostles as decribed in Acts, and completed symbolically in the coming of the gospel to Rome (Acts 28). The constant detailing of God's working to accomplish this through dreams; visions; the concatenation of circumstances (cf. the holy family's journey to Bethlehem, required by Roman law, just prior to Jesus' birth); and even hostile acts (cf. the martyrdom of Stephen; the vacillation of the Roman authorities in Palestine and the transfer of Paul's case to Rome) all converge to achieve God's purpose, as the author of Luke-Acts perceives it.

Literarily, Luke is guided by at least three models in his two-volume work. The basic structure of his Gospel derives from Mark, of course. But it is importantly transformed by combining Gospel with Hellenistic biography. As we have seen, the Gospel genre originated as a foundation document for an eschatologically oriented sect: early Christians fulfilling their mission and guiding the inner life of their esoteric community in the interim before the end of the age. The biography, on the other hand, had a long evolving history prior to the time when it began to exert influence on the Gospel form. Although we did not give attention to these factors, Matthew was also strongly

affected by the biographical tradition, especially in his
interests in the circumstances of Jesus' birth and infancy.
In Luke, however, the impact of Hellenistic and Roman
biography is clearly and pervasively apparent.

In antiquity the biography was not a fixed literary type.
The origins of the biography lie in the Greek practice of
offering an encomium to honor a worthy man at his death.
Although these funeral eulogies follow a roughly chronological sequence, with praise for ancestry and with anec-
dotes of childhood and family, the main interest is to
praise a life, rather than to portray a personality or recount
the development of a career.[27] In the Hellenistic period,
gossipy or scandalous tales were sometimes included, as
the writer became more interested in engaging his readers than in edifying them through reporting the virtuous
deeds and words of the biographical subject. The Roman
writers developed their own style of eulogy for the departed great, especially in the realms of learning, literature, or national leadership. The arrangement of the biography was much more nearly topical than chronological,
influenced by the practice of erecting public records of
the deeds of the great, as in the *Index rerum gestarum* of
Augustus. Scenes often included are those of old age and
the death of the hero; both the conceptual model and the
literary model go back to Socrates, the archetypal man of
wisdom and courage. But as D. R. Stuart has observed, the
best of the Roman biographers have produced lives of
their subjects that come much closer to modern biography
than did the Greek prototypes, in that the Romans assume
that "posterity will wish to know, for the sake of knowing,
specific things about the hero, will desire to picture him
and his environment, not merely to admire him. Certain
data owe their presence to the informatory motive
only."[28]

Charles H. Talbert has carried out a carefully re-
searched survey and analysis of the biographical form in
the Greco-Roman world.[29] Avoiding the common pitfall of
treating the Gospel as a fixed genre,[30] Talbert makes a
strong case for the influence of this biographical model on
such details of the Gospels as supernatural circumstances
of birth, ascension at the end of the career, wisdom and
benefactions as evidence of being destined for immortality.[31] Although he wants to claim all the Gospels for this
genre, his evidence and his remarks in passing point to
Luke-Acts as the New Testament writing most closely akin
to the model.[32] And Talbert acknowledges that the model
of the divinized wise man/benefactor achieves its full
statement only in the second and third centuries A.D.,
especially at the hands of Philostratus in his *Life of Apollonius of Tyana.* There is no question that there are antecedents, but Mark does not fit the model, and only Luke-
Acts includes the succession narrative, which is an
important feature of the developed pattern.[33] The mythological background and the cultic setting of the tradition
(Baptism, preaching, Eucharist, regular assemblies for
worship) are attested explicitly and fully in Luke, while
they remain at most implicit in the other Synoptic Gospels.

What has happened is that in the process of creating his
twofold work, Luke-Acts, the author has effected the
transformation of both pagan and Christian literary structures: "That which generates the new form, and at the
same time identifies it, is a new purpose or ideal, which
acts from without upon that which is traditional. . . . What
the old form supplies is not motivation or causation, or
inspiration, but only a loose structural pattern and building materials of one kind and another that may be used at
will."[34] The author of Luke-Acts is familiar with the writ-

ing of history and the composing of speeches, as practiced
by Hellenistic writers. He knows there is an audience
ready to hear stories of compassion, angelic announce-
ments of divine actions in human affairs. He is aware that
the romance—ancient equivalent of the modern novel—
has enormous popular appeal, and that its stock ingredients often include lengthy pilgrimages on religious mis-
sions, encounters with mobs and conflicts with authorities,
visits to renowned sights (such as the temple of Artemis in
Ephesus or the Agora in Athens), voyages and shipwrecks.
Most of these features are found in the early-second-century romance attributed to Xenophon of Ephesus;[35] all of
them are found in the early-second-century work known
as Luke-Acts.

Talbert is correct in his recognition of the fact that the
didactic lives of philosophers, especially in the second and
later centuries A.D., could serve as community foundation
documents. "By telling about the life of a philosopher or
ruler in terms of these specific mythologies [i.e., the myths
of ascending, apotheosized benefactors or wise men, and
of descending-ascending redeemer figures], his history
was transformed into a myth of origins which explained
the existence of a community and gave a direction for the
life of the community in the present."[36] What Talbert has
not taken adequately into account, however, is the fact
that Mark's Gospel functions as a community foundation
document in a sharply different social and cultural milieu
from Luke's; that each represents an importantly different
view of God, of his covenant people, and of his mode of
fulfilling his purpose.[37] Given Luke's different life world,
it is to be expected that he would transform the structure
of the Gospel as he took it over from the tradition, and also
transform the structures of various literary models, including biography, as he adapted them from the culture to

which his book was addressed.

Three other aspects of the social orientation of Luke-Acts may be mentioned. First there is the author's stance toward the state. Not content with Mark's or Paul's portrayal of Jesus (and, by extension, the Christians) as acquiescent under Roman rule and willing to meet basic obligations to the all-powerful state, Luke takes the initiative to show that whenever Jesus or the Christians were brought before civil authorities, the judgment rendered was always: innocent. As we noted earlier, that issue became increasingly serious as the Christians came to be known as those who refused to participate in the imperial cult. The effectiveness of the book of Acts as political propaganda is heightened by having Paul's martyrdom mentioned only indirectly and long in advance (Acts 20:22–38), while Paul's stay in Rome, though under military guard (Acts 28:16), allows him full freedom to carry on his work of teaching and preaching in Rome itself (Acts 28:31).

The second feature of Luke-Acts that displays a social dimension of Luke's community has already been mentioned briefly: the significant role of women. Akin to that is Luke's pervasive emphasis on the inclusion of outsiders in the circle of the followers of Jesus and Paul: Roman officers, Samaritans, the Ethiopian eunuch, the poor, and the demon-possessed. But Luke also records that in the Christian community there is room for the rich, the successful entrepreneur, the law-observing Jew, and the nonobservant Gentile convert.

Akin to this spirit of ecumenicity is the apparent attempt to bring together in cooperation and mutual understanding, if not in common conviction, persons of differing theological outlooks, as shown by the settlement of disputes in Acts, chs. 6; 10; 15; and 21. Even relationships between Jews and Christians are portrayed as including some elements of mutual understanding, as is evident from the advice of Gamaliel (Acts 5:33–39); Paul's continued practice of preaching in synagogues; and his participation in ritual practices and Temple worship (Acts 21). Together these features of Luke-Acts show that the book was written not only as a source of information and inspiration for Christians but also as a skillful propaganda document[38] with the aim of showing that the Christian movement was apolitical, promoting peace, inclusive across social, ethnic, and religious lines, culturally aware, and under divine control. As such it may even have been addressed to a secondary audience—to literate middle-class pagans.[39] In any event, it would help Christians prepare for responding to social or political opprobrium or to the attempt to dismiss them as ignoramuses or illiterates (Acts 4:13).

Two other New Testament writings which, like Luke-Acts, clearly show the influence of Hellenistic culture in style and substance, and which at the same time seek to stress certain continuities with Judaism, are the letter of James and the so-called letter to the Hebrews. In neither of these writings is there any evidence of distinctively Jewish-Christian problems such as we see reflected in both the letters of Paul and in Acts: problems concerning the observance of food laws or the practice of circumcision or other ritual requirements under Jewish law. Rather, it is simply assumed in both Hebrews and James that the church is the true Israel; the only question is how Israel's heritage is to be appropriated by the new covenant people.

"James" is so bold as to address the church as "the twelve tribes in the Dispersion" (James 1:1), although evidence within the writing itself of special Jewish interests or issues is completely lacking. There is obvious familiarity with the Old Testament, with references to Abraham and Rahab (James 2:21–25). But the language, the rhetoric, the illustrations and exhortations, have much in common with Stoic ethics. James's terms "religious" and "religion" (James 1:26–27), are never used by Paul, except once in a negative sense (Col. 2:18). The Pauline polemic against salvation by works of law is completely misunderstood by "James," and the concept of the "royal law" of conformity to the Ten Commandments replaces the more radical Pauline doctrine of grace with an ethical commonplace. Apart from occasional phrases, such as "the faith of our Lord Jesus Christ," there is nothing in the book that differentiates its outlook sharply from Hellenistic Judaism. It seems to have been the document of a segment of early Christianity that had humanitarian concerns (James 1:27), that was culturally rather sophisticated,[40] and that regarded itself as the authentic heir of Jewish ethical monotheism.

The letter to the Hebrews has only the external features of a letter, and is actually a treatise. Its kinship is with Hellenistic Judaism, but it seems to have been addressed to Christians. In Hebrews, as in James, none of the issues that in Paul's day divided Jewish from Gentile Christians is raised. The writer and his readers know the Septuagint as their Bible, and they share the method of interpreting the Scripture that is best attested from Alexandria: allegorical in method, Platonic in ontology. In his emphasis on faith, and on Christ as the agent of redemption and guarantor of the new covenant, the author of Hebrews resembles Paul. But in his concentration on the high-priestly role of Christ and in his warning concerning those who defect from the faith he differs considerably from Paul. More significantly, he views reality in Platonic fashion as existing at the earthly level in imperfect copies, in contrast to the heavenly archetypal realities, which are eternal (Heb. 8:1–6). Something of this distinction is present in the thought of Paul, as II Cor. 4:18 indicates, but the technical language of the philosophical system that underlies the distinction is never used by Paul, for whom *hypostasis* is merely "confidence" (II Cor. 9:4; 11:17). But in Hebrews the contrast between shadow and *hypostasis* and the importance of proof *(elenchos)* are basic to the rational argument that the Jewish cultus is good, but that it has found its ideal fulfillment in the sacrifice of Christ in the eternal sanctuary in the heavens (Heb. 9:24 to 10:10). The sophistication of the Greek rhetoric, the adroitness of the allegorical exegesis, and the facility in using the technical language of later Platonic thought—all disclose a writer whose own training and whose readers' cultural background are higher than those of any other New Testament writer. The work is an admirable forerunner of the brilliant intellectual accomplishments of the Alexandrian Christians Clement and Origen, and of Augustine of Hippo. Its genius lies not in the accommodation of the Christian tradition to Hellenistic models, but in the transformation of the literary and conceptual structures of the world of the Roman empire at the turn of the second century to serve the specific aims of certain segments of the church in their effort to engage thoughtful pagans and, if possible, to persuade them of the truth of the Christian claims.

## IV

An important strand in the New Testament writings, and one that recalls a perennial and pervasive dimension of religious life in the Greco-Roman world, is that of mysticism. The essence of mystical religion is the direct encounter with the divine, and the transforming effects that follow. In his discussion of *ekstasis* in the biblical tradition, A. Oepke recalls the fear and astonishment that the mystic experiences in the presence of the numinous. The classic figure in the Old Testament is the prophet, whom God confronts directly or whom he empowers by his Spirit to fulfill the divine purpose. That will is conveyed by the efficacious word of God, which is granted to the prophet. In postexilic times, the communication often took place in the form of ecstatic visions, the prototype of which was the vision of Isaiah in the Temple (Isa. 6). With the visions of Ezekiel, emphasis falls on the transcendent: Yahweh can be described only by analogy—Ezek. 1: "the likeness," "the appearance," "as it were"—and by elaborate symbolic imagery employed to depict the future judgment on the nations, on faithless Israel, and on God's adversary (Satan?), who is destroyed through his own pride (Ezek. 38–39). Finally there is depicted the restoration of the judged, purified nation (Ezek. 37) and of the Temple (Ezek. 40ff.). Here, of course, is the foundation on which Jewish apocalyptic was to build.[41] The next stage is evident in Daniel, where visions of the future are granted through visions and dreams. But one dimension of this literature should be distinguished from the apocalypticism as such: the mystical experience of the seer (Ezek. 1; Dan. 10). Both Ezekiel and Daniel fall prostrate in the divine presence; both are commanded to arise and to convey the God-given message to the people. In Ezekiel's situation, the whole nation is to be addressed, whether it will heed the word or not (Ezek. 2:3–7): Daniel, however, is to seal up his revelation: only the purified, the refined, the wise shall understand (Dan. 12:9–10).

This prophetic theme developed in Judaism in two different directions. The first, that of apocalypticism, as we have already seen, contributed to the formation of that segment of early Christianity which produced Mark and Revelation. The other direction was that of mysticism, as has been shown by Gershom Scholem's studies.[42] Apocalypticists and mystics were agreed on the centrality of what Martin Hengel has called "higher wisdom by revelation,"[43] and they shared the conviction that this knowledge was reserved for the circle of the elect.[44] Their crucial disagreements were on the locus and focus of revelation. For the apocalypticists, revelation was given only in and for the end time, as a way of preparing the elect to share in the life of the age to come.[45] For the mystic, there is a tension with both historical revelation and the hope for fulfillment of revelatory promises within the historical sphere. As Scholem has observed, "with no thought of denying Revelation as a fact of history, the mystic still conceives the source of religious knowledge and experience which bursts forth from the heart as being of equal importance for the conception of religious truth. . . . Instead of the one act of Revelation, there is a constant repetition of the act."[46] The conversion of eschatology of the world into eschatology of the self is described in the words of Charles A. Bennett, quoted approvingly by Scholem: "The mystic as it were forestalls the processes of history by anticipating in his own life the enjoyment of the last age."[47] While the mystic may not deny or denigrate the cosmic fulfillment of eschatological hope, his focus of interest is on the timeless mystical experience within.

A corollary of the transformation of eschatological structures among mystics is the interpretative method by which ancient documents are appropriated for present understanding. The public revelation, such as that at Sinai, has yet to unfold its meaning, and this secret meaning is the real and decisive one.[48] The meanings are secret in two senses: the secret doctrines treat "of the most deeply hidden and fundamental matters of human life";[49] but they are also secret in that they are "confined to a small elite who impart the knowledge to their disciples." The mystical conventicle, in its interpretation of the traditional texts, may engage in allegorical exegesis, but the penetration to the deeper meaning is through symbolic perception: "In the mystic symbol a reality which in itself has, for us, no form or shape becomes transparent, and, as it were, visible through the medium of another reality which clothes its content with visible and expressible meaning."[50] Although Scholem is speaking of the Kabbala, his delineation of the hermeneutical method is relevant for the earlier periods of Jewish mysticism as well: the approach by mystic symbolism "discovers something else which is not covered by the allegorical network: a reflection of the true transcendence. The symbol 'signifies' nothing and communicates nothing, but makes something transparent which is beyond all expression."[51]

Since Jewish exegesis subsequent to the destruction of the Second Temple was wholly dominated by the rabbis, with their halakhic and haggadic methods, the mystical tradition was suppressed and its literature all but disappeared or was taken over by the Christians. Among these mystical documents nearly lost to the Jewish community are the Apocalypse of Abraham,[52] the so-called III Enoch,[53] and the Testament of Job.[54] The divine throne-chariot figures in the fragmentary Angelic Liturgy from Qumran, which pictures the spirits of the living God as moving perpetually with the glory of the wonderful chariot.[55] The goal of the faithful was the mystical ascent; in the divine presence, illuminated by the divine radiance, the worshiper was transfigured.

This kind of religious aspiration was by no means limited

to Jews of this period. The traditions about Orpheus as mystagogue probably developed at Athens in the sixth century B.C. and had by the fifth century become a pattern of life (involving abstinence from meat, from woolen clothing, and from contact with birth or death; expectation of a future life through initiation and discipline in this life). However, evidence for the formation of Orphic communities is scant and ambiguous until imperial times.[56] The potential was there for building a sense of brotherhood and of a *cosmopolis* through the underlying notions of the unity of the race, of the gods, and of mystical experience.[57] It was the belief of the Orphics that they were coming to the end of the cycle of reincarnations, and that they would then pass beyond Elysium to the highest spiritual abode, among the stars.[58] The specific hope of spiritual ascent is attested in an oration of Aristides, in which he reports how he was healed through a vision of Sarapis and Asclepius, who first cured him of a head ailment, and then enabled him to see "ladders which mark the boundary between the upper world and the nether world." Becoming aware that Sarapis was able to convey human beings without vehicles and apart from their bodies, he rose up the ladder by means of the mystic rites and was transformed.[59]

As we noted briefly in Chapter 2, Isis became a major religious figure in the early empire because of her combined roles of guarantor of cosmic order and compassionate benefactress to the sick and needy. Diodorus Siculus in his *Library of History* tells how Osiris turned over to Isis the supreme power (17.3), and placed at her side Hermes, who was the discerner of the harmony of the stars and of music (16.1). She discovered health-giving drugs and developed the science of healing. She "finds her greatest delight in the healing of mankind and gives aid in their sleep to those who call upon her, plainly manifesting both her presence and her beneficence towards humans who ask her help. . . . For standing above the sick in their sleep she gives them aid for their diseases and works remarkable cures upon such as submit themselves to her; and many who have been despaired of by their physicians because of the difficult nature of their malady are restored to health by her, while numbers who have altogether lost the use of their eyes or some other part of the body, whenever they turn for help to this goddess are restored to their previous condition" (25.2–5).[60] The testimonies to Asclepius, the chief healing god among the Greeks since Homeric times,[61] report similar visits to his shrine, the sacrifices and prayers, incubation in his temple, the epiphany of the deity, the subsequent cure, and the offering of thanks.[62] Aretalogies from shrines of Sarapis bear nearly identical testimony to the healing power of the god.[63] The enormous appeal of these healing shrines lay not only in the cures they provided[64] but also in the religious experience of direct communion with deity. The deep devotion to Isis is perceptible in the romance by Xenophon of Ephesus, where narrative details reflect the Isis cult and where the relationship between the lovers parallels that of Isis and Osiris.[65] Deep religious sentiments are expressed in the familiar words of Apuleius in praise of Isis:

> O holy and blessed dame, the perpetual comfort of human kind, who by Thy bounty and grace nourishest all the world, and bearest a great affection to the adversities of the miserable as a loving mother, Thou takest no rest night or day, neither art Thou idle at any time in giving benefits and succouring all men as well on land as sea; Thou art she that puttest away all storms and dangers from men's life by stretching forth Thy right hand.

After describing her control over the universe, over destiny, the reverence which she enjoys among the gods above and below, the fertility of plants and animals which she makes possible, he acknowledges the inadequacy of his words to offer her appropriate praise.

> Howbeit as a good religious person, and according to my poor estate, I will do what I may: I will always keep Thy divine appearance in remembrance, and close the imagination of Thy most holy godhead within my breast.[66]

The mystical experience linked with both Jewish and wider Hellenistic tradition is evident in the New Testament at several points. Some aspects, such as the heavenly vision, the transfiguration by the divine radiance, the assurance of vindication, are apparent in the Gospel story of the transfiguration of Jesus,[67] as well as in Paul's oblique and compressed mention of his mystical transport in II Cor. 12.[68] It is in the Gospel of John, however, that the convergence of religious phenomena we have been considering in this section is most evident.

John's Gospel opens with a kind of hymn to the preexistent Logos, who is the agent of creation and the savior of all who turn to him in trust. If the author had not been required by the sex of Jesus to employ a masculine term, *logos,* he could well have used the feminine word, *sophia,* which would have made the kinship between his *logos* teaching and Jewish wisdom doctrine the more evident. But as we observed in Chapter 2, the image that helped to shape the Jewish image of wisdom, creatrix and benefactress, was that of Isis. Persons moved by the Christian equivalent of the kind of piety that characterized the followers of Isis were those who seem to have been drawn to the Johannine portrayal of Jesus. The Christian adaptation of this mystical mode of religiosity is everywhere evident in John.

Before looking more closely at the Johannine elements that resemble those of the Isis mysteries, we need to bear in mind one fact that distinguishes this Gospel from the Isis mythology: John has stressed the historical reality of the savior figure whom he depicts. The Logos hymn itself is interrupted by references to John the Baptist, the historical personage through whom Jesus was led into public activity. Jesus' human paternity is stressed ("son of Joseph," John 1:45) as is his earthly birthplace, Nazareth (1:45). Commentators have long noted the human limitations attributed to Jesus in John, such as weariness and thirst (4:6), deception (7:8–10), and grief (11:35). Most telling of all are his subjection to the authorities in Jerusalem, his death and burial. Clearly John means "was made flesh" literally, not as a divine masquerade. Even the risen Christ is portrayed as tangible and corporeal, as the invitation to see and feel the wounds attests (20:27). For John, Jesus is not a mythical figure from the past, but a historical person of recent times. That conviction does not prevent John, however, from employing the imagery and rhetoric of Hellenistic myth and mystery in his representation of Jesus as the sole revealer of God: "No one has seen God at any time; a unique divine one, who is in the bosom of the Father, he has made him known" (1:18).[69]

Three aspects of John's Gospel manifest his mystical piety, especially of the kind linked with Isis. The first is the importance attached to the new beginning that is granted to the faithful. In Apuleius' testimony, his bodily transformation from ass to man is matched by the inward affective change, symbolized by his new garments, the lighted torch he bears, and the wonder with which he is greeted by the fellow members of the "holy order" into which he has been initiated. The new birth and its contrast to ordinary human birth are mentioned in the opening part of John's prologue; the outcome of that experience of faith is to "become children of God" (1:12–13). The theme of the new birth is given its fullest exposition—though in intentionally ambiguous and provocative language—in Jesus' conversation with Nicodemus, a ruler of the Jews and the teacher of Israel (3:10). Jews are thereby depicted as those who claim to be God's people but who do not comprehend his purpose. Membership in God's people is open to all, but participation is possible only through the Spirit, not by ancestry or logic. The inclusiveness of the people of God is evident in the response of the Samaritans (4:39) to the testimony of the converted wanton woman at the well and in the seeking Greeks of John 12. In veiled but polemical language, Jesus is reported as redefining the true descendants of Abraham (ch. 8), the true flock of God (ch. 10), and the true vine (ch. 15). Though the discourse on the Vine builds on imagery from the prophets (Isa. 5:1–7; Jer. 2:21; Ezek. 19:10–14), the focus is on the organic unity of the vine and branches—in short, the mystical union of the Revealer and his own faithful people. The language of mystical communion ("continue in me, and I in you," 15:4), with its stress on love (15:9–11), would be wholly comprehensible to followers of Isis. The goal of mystical unity is explicit in John 17:22–23, where the divine radiance is transmitted to the faithful, who are one among themselves, one with the Revealer, and one with God: "that they may become perfectly one."

We have already touched on another feature of John which closely resembles that of the Isis cult (noted briefly in Chapter 3): the self-pronouncements of the Revealer. In the inscriptions and literary remains that contain statements in praise of Isis, her beneficences are at times described in the third person, but often she addresses her worshipers in the first person ("I am Isis, who . . ."). In the Isis aretalogies, her virtues *(aretai)* are praised with regard to her role as agent and sustainer of creation as well as in connection with her specific acts of kindness in healing the ill who have come to her for help.[70] In John, the self-pronouncements of Jesus are nearly always followed by a functional description, and in some cases are linked with his miracles. For example, the first of the "I am" sayings is in John 6:35, which ties in with the miraculous feeding just recounted (6:1–12). Jesus' identity as "bread of life" is paralleled by the promise, "whoever comes to me shall not hunger; whoever believes in me shall never thirst." The intervening material, following the narrative of the miracle itself, has placed the discussion of its meaning against the background of the miraculous feeding of Israel in the desert of Sinai (6:31–33). Obviously, what is at issue is not physical sustenance but spiritual participation in the true covenant people: those who see in Jesus the revelatory agent of God (6:33). What is required is not merely intellectual assent, but participation: "Whoever eats of this bread will live for ever" (6:51). The declaration, "I am the resurrection and the life" (11:25) and the matching challenge/promise, "whoever believes in me . . . shall live," are likewise linked with a miracle, the raising of Lazarus from the dead (ch. 11). These words are not merely informational, but are aimed at promoting faith in the community of his followers (11:42). Thus the accounts of personal benefits received in the miracles combine with the "I am" declarations of Jesus to build up the community of faith. The status of that community is threatened by those whose prosaic hearing of the words of Jesus leads them to think he speaks nonsense (cf. Nicodemus in 3:4), and by those whose religious convictions find his claims blasphemous (8:59), as well as by those who regard him and his movement as a threat to the social and political stability of the Jewish people (11:47–53). The Jesus movement is portrayed in John as beleaguered, but its constituents find mutual support and encouragement in its meetings and meals of mystical communion (chs. 13–17). The initial postresurrection appearances of Jesus are at gatherings behind closed doors (20:19, 26). They were warned: "I have given them thy word, and the world has hated them because they are not of the world, even as I am not of the world."

It is in keeping with this understanding of the Christian community as a conventicle of the faithful that the Johannine Jesus addresses his own in the other "I am" sayings. He proclaims, "I am the light of the world" (8:12), but it is only those who follow him who will perceive the light and walk in its illuminating path. "I am the door. . . . I am the good shepherd" (10:7, 11), says Jesus, but only those who heed his voice, who enter his flock by faith, will be saved. All the others will find it impossible to understand what he is saying to them (10:6). "I am the way, and the truth, and the life" (14:6), and there is no way to God except through him. After his death, the world will be unable to see him, but *they* will see him (14:19); *they* will share in his works (14:12), his love (14:15), his peace (14:27), which the world outside the community can neither provide nor experience. His followers cannot escape persecution (15:18–25), because their proclamation of his word will bring conviction, guilt, and retaliation, as did his own preaching. It is the Spirit that he will send to the community that will provide the basis of its understanding of the divine will (16:12–15). They are to live through the tribulation and hostility of the world in confidence of ultimate vindication ("Be of good cheer, I have overcome the

world," 16:33) and of final removal from the world (14:3).
The mingling of elements of both Merkabah mysticism
and Isis piety is evident, as well as John's transformation
of both.

The mystical insights of the community are apparent in
yet another dimension of the Gospel of John: the miracle
stories. For these John prefers the term "signs" (2:11; 20:
30–31). They are recounted, not merely for information,
but to convert and to edify: "that you may believe ..." The
meaning of the stories is not simply that they are evidence
of supernatural powers or of Jesus' divine origin. Their
import is discernible only to his faithful disciples (2:11),
who alone believe in him when his "glory" is manifest
through the signs. As in the mystical exegesis described by
Gershom Scholem (see above), the stories depict more
than the satisfying of day-to-day needs (food and drink) or
the solution of health problems (the lame, the blind). The
imagery of water, wine, and food conceals for the outsider
but reveals to the insider the spiritual meaning of Christ
and the resources he offers to his own. Water is a spring
welling up to eternal life (4:14). The bread and wine
miraculously supplied are the food and drink of eternal life
(6:55). The restoration of sight to the blind and the hostility
of the religious leaders are signs of divine judgment: "For
judgment I came into this world, that those who do not see
may see, and that those who see may become blind" (9:
39).[71]

The esoteric quality of the Johannine community is further evident in the Gospel's delight in the use of words of
double meaning. Thus, to be born *anōthen* (3:3ff.) can
mean to be born a second time ("again") or "from above"
—that is, to be born of God, as declared in 1:13. When
Jesus predicts that he will be "lifted up from the earth,"
the prophecy could concern his crucifixion (12:32) or his

exaltation into the presence of God, as 12:32 implies. Similar ambiguity is present in Pilate's question to Jesus,
"Where are you from?" (19:9), and in the question raised
by the Pharisees about Jesus' age (8:56–58). Inability to
perceive who Jesus is or to comprehend his words is not
a matter of lack of information or of spiritual insight: "He
who walks in the darkness does not know where he goes.
While you have the light, believe in the light, that you may
become sons of light" (12:35–36).

In the letters of John there is a similar outlook: sharing
in the revelation through Christ is the ground of participation in the Father and the Son (I John 1:1–3). The imagery
and the affective appeal are much the same, as is the
sectarian consciousness of the community behind the Johannine epistles: "They went out from us, but they were
not of us; for if they had been of us, they would have
continued with us. . . . But you have been anointed by the
Holy One, and you all know" (I John 2:19–20). II John
affirms the importance of mutual love as the ground for
sharing in the community, it warns against those whose
doctrinal aberration is ground for exclusion: "If any one
comes to you and does not bring this doctrine, do not
receive him into the house or give him any greeting."
Thus II John conveys the impression of a group that finds
its unity in common conviction and mutual love, akin
therefore to the atmosphere presented in John 13:35: "By
this all men will know that you are my disciples, if you
have love for one another."[72]

V

In II and III John, however, the "truth" is assumed to
have strongly conceptual aspects, rather than the person-
alized "truth" of John 14:6. In the passage from II John

quoted above, and even more clearly in the expression "follow the truth" (II John 4; III John 3), an important criterion for acceptance within the community is right doctrine, or what later comes to be orthodoxy. Akin to this is the requirement to acknowledge and be subject to ecclesiastical authority, as the put-down of Diotrephes (III John 9–10) shows. By the early third century, the attempt to correlate revealed truth through Christ with the insights of the philosophers reached a high point in Origen's commentary on—not surprisingly—the Gospel of John. For Origen, the hidden truth of God was not so much mystical knowledge to be safeguarded within the esoteric group (as in John); it was insight concealed from the literalistic reader of Scripture but disclosed to those who used the spiritual or allegorical method of interpretation. Without negating the devotional dimensions of the study of Scripture, exegesis became for Origen an intellectual, even an academic challenge. His philosophical moorings were provided by the Platonic tradition; his interpretative methods were largely derived from the tradition best known from the works of Philo, also of Alexandria.[73]

In describing his exegetical method, Origen sounds very much like the Johannine mystic: "Our whole effort is now to be directed to the effort to penetrate to the deep things of the meaning of the gospel and to search out the truth that is in them . . ." Just as the Word was made flesh in Jesus and then returned to God in the Spirit, so the Word of Scripture must be viewed, not in terms of its somatic surface, but its spiritual inner meaning.[74] When, however, Origen becomes specific about what spiritual exegesis requires, his bench mark is Plato as taught in Alexandria in his day.[75] The pattern for this process, which was laid down in Philo, is prepared for in the later letters of John, especially in the mingling of mystic participation and the conceptualization of truth.

Both the consolidation of doctrine and the concentration of ecclesiastical authority are even more forcefully at work in the pastoral letters, as we have noted. Using the outward form of the Pauline letter, even to the point of including what appear to be occasional, purely personal remarks—such as when the absentminded apostle asks help in retrieving the books he has left behind (II Tim. 4:13)—these pseudo letters are wielded as instruments to bring about doctrinal conformity and submission to authority. The church is beset by heretics, who wander away into vain discussion (I Tim. 1:6); give heed to doctrines of demons (I Tim. 4:1); have a morbid craving for controversy (I Tim. 6:4); and hold the form of religion but deny the power of it (II Tim. 3:5); will listen to anybody and can never arrive at a knowledge of the truth (II Tim. 3:7). To make matters worse, their morals are as bad as their theology (II Tim. 3:1–6). The "pattern of sound words" by which the truth has been transmitted from the apostle is to be preserved: "Guard the truth that has been entrusted to you" (II Tim. 1:14). Thus the letter has become the instrument of doctrinal, moral, and ecclesiastical control in a community that is increasingly secular. Its public gatherings are plagued by embarrassing ostentation on the part of wealthy women (I Tim. 2:9) and by vain disputes, moral laxness, and inflated egos (I Tim. 3:6)—in short, the church is a mixed bag (II Tim. 2:20). Boredom with the familiar has led some to the excitement of speculation (I Tim. 4:7; II Tim. 4:3–4). What is required, "Paul" is made to declare, is solidity, respectability, concern for public image, acceptance of and perseverance in church leadership roles, even those of a more menial sort (I Tim. 3:8ff.; 5:9ff.). Like the author of the letter to the Ephesians, the

writer of the pastoral letters was "eager to maintain the
unity of the Spirit in the bond of peace" (Eph. 4:3), but the
striving for unity seems to the modern reader a hopeless
goal for a community as fragmented as the one he here
addresses. Although the threat of persecution is mentioned (II Tim. 1:16–17; 2:9; 4:6–7), the church of the pastorals seems more in danger from inner strife than from
outside attack.


## VI

Just as Judaism did not draw the limits of its canon of
Scripture until it was in a situation of relative tranquillity
following the defeat of Jewish nationalists by the Romans
in the first revolt, so the Christians did not draw up a
widely agreed upon definitive list of Christian scriptures
until after Christianity had been officially sanctioned by
the imperial authorities. As was the case in Judaism, a
major motivation was the desire to exclude from use in the
congregations books that were regarded as heretical by
the dominant religious authorities. Surely a major factor in
the Jewish formulation of a canon at Jamnia in the 90's was
the Christians' exploitation of and additions to the Jewish
scriptures. In the second and subsequent centuries the
Christians had to set forth their standard list of New Testament scriptures in order to achieve centralization of doctrinal authority.

For nearly a century after the crucifixion, Christians
seem to have preferred the oral tradition about Jesus to
the written Gospels. Papias, bishop of Hierapolis (ca. 60–
130), declared that his esteem was higher for what came
through "the living voice"[76]—that is, from those who had
heard the apostles, who in turn had heard Jesus—than for
what was written down in books. The Gospels themselves

built on oral traditions, including pronouncements made
in Jesus' name after his death, but considered to be of
equal authority with his remembered words because they
had been given by the Spirit from the living Lord. Sayings
"of the Lord" continued to circulate orally even after the
Gospels had begun to record them in fixed form. As the
tradition proliferated, however, more and more books
were written purporting to be the records of Jesus and his
followers. Certain Gospels attributed to the apostles (Matthew, John) or to their companions (Mark, Luke) began to
be read liturgically in Christian worship, along with the
Old Testament, with the result that the New Testament
writings began to assume a normative quality. This esteem
was reinforced by the practice of church leaders in referring to the New Testament writings by the same respect-
ful formulas ("scripture says"; "it is written") that were
used for the Old Testament. With other writings pressing
their claims to a place alongside the letters of Paul and
what came to be considered the four canonical Gospels, it
was inevitable that choices had to be made among them.
But by what criteria?

By the middle of the second century Justin was speaking
of the "memoirs" of the apostles, by which he meant our
four Gospels, and it was the traditional link each was
thought to have with an apostle that lent them their authority. About the same time, Marcion took a different
route: he recognized only the Gospel of Luke and the
letters of Paul, but he rejected the Old Testament as Scripture for Christians. His criteria were theological: Paul's
doctrine of justification by faith was the central Christian
teaching, so that only his letters and the one Gospel (in a
slightly expurgated version) written by Paul's companion
could be normative for true Christians.

By the late second century, a clear consensus had begun

to emerge, as expressed by the three great theologians of the end of that century, Clement of Alexandria, Irenaeus, and Tertullian. Living in different parts of the Mediterranean world, and being of very different temperament and theological outlook, Irenaeus in Gaul, Tertullian in Africa, and Clement in Egypt simply agree that the church has received four Gospels, the Pauline letters, and the other, so-called catholic, or general, epistles. Other writings attributed to apostles, such as the Gospel of Thomas and the Gospel of Peter, were excluded. There is no absolute agreement about certain books, such as the letters of John and Revelation, but the central core is fixed. By what reasoning? Irenaeus merely asserts that, as there are four winds, and four parts of the world, so there are four Gospels.

As we should expect, there were attempts to alter this list, through combining the four Gospels into one (Tatian's Diatessaron) and through adding other Gospels (especially by the Gnostics). And a more elaborate rationale for including these writings and no others was offered by Origen.[77] But when in the early fourth century Eusebius of Caesarea, adviser to Constantine and archivist of early Christian history, drew up the official list, it was nearly identical with the present collection of twenty-seven writings. Only Revelation was under dispute, and it appears that even Eusebius could not make up his mind on that issue.[78] Practically speaking, then, the church had a normative list of scriptures from the middle of the second century forward, based largely on the claim that they were all apostolically authored or authorized.

What occurred, therefore, in the emergence of the canon of the New Testament was not in the first instance a theological development. Indeed, the theological differences among the various books that came to be included

in the New Testament were largely ignored in the drive
to form a canon and thereby to exclude certain writings
from the list that the church was to regard as authoritative.
Yet in the process of achieving this normative list of Christian scriptures the church was overlooking or intentionally
blocking out the social and cultural diversity of its own
past as it moved into an epoch in which unity of faith and
practice would be regarded as the indispensable ground of
survival and growth. The evidence for tracing the history
of the canon is spotty and ambiguous, and need not be
traced here.[79] It is important for our purposes, however,
to note those factors which made the canon-building both
possible and necessary.

The penetration of the Christian movement into the
more sophisticated strata of Roman society and the attraction that it had for persons capable of both administrative
and intellectual leadership made possible the construction
of ecclesiastical and theological structures built on the
premise that unity makes for strength. The proliferation
of groups claiming to be Christian, while affirming notions
that the mainstream regarded as unacceptable, demanded
that there be norms for distinguishing truth from error.
For this purpose there were the personal authorities embodied in the bishops as well as the external authorities set
forth in creeds and canon. The social dimensions of the
canon are apparent in the determination to lend authority
to the writings by tracing them back to the circle of those
originally authorized by Jesus: the apostles, and their immediate associates. As the living memories of village-
based, charismatic-led Christianity faded, and as Christianity became increasingly a bourgeois phenomenon, the
social and cultural differences that had characterized the
movement from the outset were blended into structures
that presented the appearance of uniformity. The histori-

cal differences in origins were no longer important; what mattered was a united front against heretics and other hostile forces. The canon was a valuable aid toward the achievement of this kind of unity.

Still later the growth of ecclesiastical structures, fostered by the central authority of the empire from the fourth century on, would provide the machinery and the obligation to unite the church, organizationally and in the form of conciliar pronouncements. But it is grossly anachronistic to read the fourth-century unity—qualified though it was—back into the first and early second centuries. As we seek to discern the complexities of the process of the origins of Christianity, and to discover the variety of responses that the story of Jesus elicited in the Greco-Roman culture of the early empire, our quest is facilitated by the analytical methods developed in the social sciences.

Our sources are too sparse and scattered for us to discover who the anonymous persons were who wrote most of these ancient Christian books. We cannot identify all those who transformed the social and literary structures of their situation, doing so in order to interpret for their committed colleagues what God was saying to the human race through Jesus, and to create the communities in which that myth and ritual would be preserved. But then we began our study by acknowledging, with Prof. Cadbury, that we were not so much interested in who they were as in how they "got that way."

# NOTES

## 1. INTRODUCTION

1. H. J. Cadbury, "Current Issues in New Testament Study," *Harvard Divinity School Bulletin,* Vol. 19 (1953), p. 54.

2. Cadbury's fundamental work, *The Making of Luke-Acts,* 2d ed. (Alec R. Allenson, 1958), is still in print, as is the multivolume study of Acts to which he contributed, *The Beginnings of Christianity,* 5 vols., ed. by F. J. Foakes-Jackson, K. Lake, and H. J. Cadbury (repr., Baker Book House, 1965).

3. Eusebius, *Ecclesiastical History* III.39.

4. Eusebius, *Orat. Const.* II.5. The exploitation of the biblical image of the ark discloses how Eusebius saw empire and church as correlative instruments of divine purpose.

5. F. C. Baur, "Die Christuspartei in der korinthischen Gemeinde, der Gegensatz des petrinischen und paulinischen Christenthums in der ältesten Kirche, der Apostel Petrus in Rom," *Tübinger Zeitschrift für Theologie,* Vol. 4 (1831), pp. 61ff.

6. Discussed and demonstrated by Werner Georg Kümmel, *The New Testament: The History of the Investigation of Its Problems,* tr. by S. M. Gilmour and H. C. Kee (Abingdon Press, 1972), pp. 130–143.

7. F. C. Baur, in Kümmel, *The New Testament,* p. 133.

8. The title used here translates the original, *Das Wesen des Christentums* (Leipzig, 1901); the English translation by T. B. Saunders was assigned the less appropriate title, *What Is Christianity?* (Harper & Brothers [1901], 1957).

9. Tr. in Kümmel, *The New Testament,* pp. 182–183.

10. In *Jesus and the Word,* tr. by E. H. Lantero and L. P. Smith (Charles Scribner's Sons, 1934), pp. 3–4, 11, 47–48.

11. Details in Rudolf Bultmann, *The Gospel of John* (German

editions, 1947, 1957; suppl., 1966); Eng. tr. by G. R. Beasley-
Murray et al. (Westminster Press, 1971). The theological results
of the emended John are evident in Bultmann's *Theology of the
New Testament,* tr. by Kendrick Grobel, Vol. II (Charles
Scribner's Sons, 1955).

12. Rudolf Bultmann, *Primitive Christianity in Its Contemporary Setting,* tr. by R. H. Fuller (Meridian Books, 1956). The rise
of the Gnostic redeemer hypothesis is traced in Kümmel, *The
New Testament,* pp. 350–360, and is analyzed critically by Car-
sten Colpe in *Die religionsgeschichtliche Schule* (Göttingen:
Vandenhoeck & Ruprecht, 1961). Bultmann's misuse of rabbinic
material is exposed by Jacob Neusner in *The Rabbinic Traditions
About the Pharisees Before 70* (Leiden: E. J. Brill, 1971), Vol. III,
pp. 362–363.

13. Martin Dibelius, *Die Formgeschichte des Evangeliums*
(1919; 2d ed., 1933); Eng. tr. by B. L. Woolf: *From Tradition to
Gospel* (Charles Scribner's Sons, 1935; repr. Attic Press, 1972).
Rudolf Bultmann, *Die Geschichte der synoptischen Tradition*
(1921); Eng. tr. by John Marsh: *The History of the Synoptic Tradition* (Harper & Brothers, 1963).

In 1970 Erhardt Güttgemanns published a detailed analysis of
the antecedents and subsequent developments of the form-critical method: *Offene Fragen zur Formgeschichte des Evangeliums*
(Munich: Chr. Kaiser Verlag, 1970). In it he sought to show (1)
that the Gospels as literary products are more than and utterly
different from the random collection of oral tradition that form
critics assumed them to be; (2) that Jewish apocalypticism produced literature, so that early Christian expectation of the imminent Parousia would not have prevented the writing of the Gospel; (3) that studies of the transmission of oral tradition disclose
very different patterns from those observable in the development of the Gospel tradition (pp. 120–153). Though these are
important and largely valid observations, they have been anticipated or even elaborated in the work of others. But Güttgemanns then declares that the only way to understand the
Gospels and their origins is as psycholinguistic phenomena. Although he goes on to speak of the *Sitze-im-Leben* of the Gospels
as the entire culture, the horizon and understanding of a cultural
circle, his detailed analysis of the Gospel tradition concentrates
almost solely on literary and preliterary aspects, with the result
that the social and cultural dimensions are largely ignored, even
though the work concludes with an appeal to take sociocultural
phenomena into account. The declaration that the Gospel is an
"auto-semantic" form that can be explained only by itself (p. 197)

would seem to make unnecessary the search for cultural antecedents or developments. The hints of detailed work on Mark in
preparation indicate a concentration on Christological questions
which will leave out of account the ethical and ritual passages
that take up so much of Mark's Gospel but which must be seen
as in some way integrated with the overall aim of Mark. (See on
this my *Community of the New Age;* Westminster Press, 1977.)
In the epilogue to the English translation of his work by W. G.
Doty *(Candid Questions Concerning Gospel Form Criticism;*
Pickwick Press, 1979), Güttgemanns refers to his book as having
stimulated a "scientific revolution" (p. 417). But if Thomas S.
Kuhn is correct that a new scientific paradigm will find acceptance only if it seems "to resolve some outstanding and generally
recognized problems that can be met in no other way" *(The
Structure of Scientific Revolutions;* 2d ed., University of Chicago
Press, 1970, p. 169; see note 26 below), then Güttgemanns' work
thus far looks more like a welcome clearing of scholarly rubble
than a revolution.

14. Richly documented by Martin Hengel, *Judaism and Hellenism,* 2 vols., tr. by John Bowden (Fortress Press, 1974).

15. Most notably by William Ramsay, as in *St. Paul the Trav-
eller and the Roman Citizen* (London, 1920). The same tradition
of learned British historical conservatism is now represented by
F. F. Bruce, *New Testament History* (Doubleday & Co., Anchor
Books, 1972). Bruce assumes that history and theology are separate enterprises, though the former has implications (un-
specified) for the latter. In using Acts as a historical source, for
example, Bruce asks about neither its reliability as a source nor
its distinctive place in the growth of early Christian literature
and life.

16. Adolf Deissmann, *Light from the Ancient East* (Eng. tr.
1910; rev. 1927; repr. Baker Book House, 1978).

17. See, e.g., Nigel Turner, "Second Thoughts: Papyrus Finds,"
*Expository Times,* Vol. 74 (1964); Edgar V. McKnight, "The New
Testament and 'Biblical Greek,' " *Journal of Bible and Religion,*
Vol. 34 (1966), pp. 36–42; H. C. Kee, "The Function of Scriptural
Quotations and Allusions," in *Jesus und Paulus,* ed. by E. E. Ellis
and E. Grässer (Göttingen: Vandenhoeck & Ruprecht, 1975), pp.
165–188, where evidence is offered from the formative influence
of the LXX on narrative details of the Markan passion story.

18. S. J. Case's most effective presentation is *The Social Origins
of Christianity* (University of Chicago Press, 1923). His earlier
work, *The Evolution of Early Christianity* (University of Chicago Press, 1914, 1942; repr. 1960), is oriented toward the reli-

gious experience of the individual; the result is long on a sophisticated analysis of personal piety but short on social dynamics.

19. Robert W. Funk, "The Watershed of the American Biblical Tradition: The Chicago School, First Phase, 1892–1920," *Journal of Biblical Literature,* Vol. 95 (1976), pp. 15–17.

20. Ibid., pp. 18–19.

21. K. O. L. Burridge, *New Heaven, New Earth: A Study of Millenarian Activities* (Schocken Books, 1969); Norman Cohn, *The Pursuit of the Millennium,* 2d ed. (Harper & Brothers, Harper Torchbooks, 1961); Peter Worsley, *The Trumpet Shall Sound,* 2d ed. (Schocken Books, 1968); Bryan Wilson, *Magic and the Millennium* (Harper & Row, 1973); Leon Festinger et al., *When Prophecy Fails* (Harper & Row, Harper Torchbooks [1956]). Significant works on sociology of knowledge and its philosophical background are discussed below, 23–26, 30–31, and listed in notes 40–50 below.

22. Peter Brown, *Religion and Society in the Age of Saint Augustine* (Harper & Row, 1972); E. R. Dodds, *Pagan and Christian in an Age of Anxiety* (Cambridge University Press, 1965).

23. Gerd Theissen, *Sociology of Early Palestinian Christianity,* tr. by John Bowden (Fortress Press, 1978), describes the dynamics of the movement as led by itinerant charismatics. Although a similar undertaking might be inferred from the title of Joachim Jeremias' *Jerusalem in the Time of Jesus: An Investigation Into Economic and Social Conditions During the New Testament Period* (tr. by F. H. and C. H. Cave; 3d ed., Fortress Press, 1969), that work is limited to a description of institutions and background conditions in Palestine, with the reader left to infer social dynamics. On the social factors in Pauline churches, Theissen's "Soziale Schichtung in der korinthischen Gemeinde," *Zeitschrift für die neutestamentliche Wissenschaft,* Vol. 65 (1974), pp. 232–272, shows the socially mixed situation among the Christians of Corinth.

24. Abraham J. Malherbe, *Social Aspects of Early Christianity* (Louisiana State University Press, 1977). The strength of Malherbe's work lies in his mastery of the primary literature of the early Roman period and his grasp of the insights of social historians of the period, especially the work of Ramsay MacMullen, *Enemies of the Roman Order* (Harvard University Press, 1966) and *Roman Social Relations* (Yale University Press, 1974). Not mentioned by Malherbe, but sociologically useful is Christopher P. Jones, *The Roman World of Dio Chrysostom* (Harvard University Press, 1978). Essays analyzing biblical material in sociological terms include Leander E. Keck, "On the Ethos of Early Chris-

tians," *Journal of the American Academy of Religion,* Vol. 42 (1974); Wayne A. Meeks, "The Man from Heaven in Johannine Sectarianism," *Journal of Biblical Literature,* Vol. 91 (1972), pp. 44–72; and "The Image of the Androgyne: Some Uses of a Symbol in Earliest Christianity," *History of Religions,* Vol. 13 (1974).

25. John G. Gager, *Kingdom and Community: The Social World of Early Christianity* (Prentice-Hall, 1975), p. 12. Gager justly complains that New Testament scholars have approached historical study of Christian origins with theological biases and with the assumption of the uniqueness of Christianity (pp. 4–6). His hope is well founded that sociological paradigms "will make it possible to see old facts in new light" (p. 11). But biases can be negative as well as positive, so that to begin with the assumption that "the Christian religion, from start to finish, is a typical expression of Greco-Roman piety" (p. 6) seems to prejudge the distinctive features of the movement and is in fact belied by Gager's final essay on "The Success of Christianity," where its unique features are traced.

26. "Paradigm" is used here in the sense employed currently in the discussion of the nature of scientific and religious language and thought. The mixture of naiveté and pathos that characterized Comte's "Religion of Humanity" has not yet disappeared: the bland assumption still operates that any evidence that cannot be corroborated by the standard methods of natural science is historically impossible. Rather than seeking to enter sympathetically the life world of persons living in an ancient culture, a contemporary historian like Morton Smith, in his *Jesus the Magician* (Harper & Row, 1978), brackets Jesus with itinerant tricksters and demoniacs of the Roman period and dismisses the reported experiences of the disciples as hallucinations (p. 121) and aspects of their psychopathic histories (p. 139). There was not, however, a single, unified life world in the early Roman world, and certainly not everyone in that epoch shared the view or views represented by the magical papyri, so that to "read the gospels with some knowledge of ancient magical material," while it may shed light on details, does not ensure a grasp of "what, in light of that material, the gospel stories and sayings really say" (p. 139). Smith is evaluating the New Testament material by his own paradigms rather than trying to discover what social construction of reality lies behind these early Christian writings.

Sensitivity as to the way in which paradigms transform the evidence of which the paradigm seeks to make sense has been evident among such eminent historians of science as Thomas S.

Kuhn, in his brilliant *The Structure of Scientific Revolutions* and among philosophers of science such as Ian G. Barbour, in *Myths, Models and Paradigms: A Comparative Study in Science and Religion* (Harper & Row, 1974). Barbour writes: "Science is not so objective as regularly represented, nor is religion so subjective. Scientific models are products of creative analogical imagination. . . . Religious paradigms, like scientific ones, are not falsified by data, but are replaced by promising alternatives" (p. 171). A paradigm "defines for a scientific community the types of questions that may legitimately be asked, the types of explanation that are to be sought, and the types of solutions that are acceptable" (p. 103).

27. Robert H. Pfeiffer, *History of New Testament Times: With an Introduction to the Apocrypha* (Harper & Brothers, 1949). Pfeiffer's separation of religious, political, and literary factors is a subjective and arbitrary choice. Furthermore, it precludes understanding of the complex factors that converged to shape primitive Christianity.

28. Reprinted in Paul Ricoeur, *History and Truth,* tr. and with an introduction by Charles A. Kelbley (Northwestern University Press, 1965).

29. Ibid., p. 123.

30. Ibid.

31. Ibid., p. 25.

32. Ibid., p. 30.

33. Here Ricoeur seems close to the hermeneutical stance of Wilhelm Dilthey, especially in his later writings. Although Dilthey is often accused of having been too beholden to the natural sciences and of having worshiped at the shrine of objectivity (see David E. Linge, in his Introduction to Hans-Georg Gadamer, *Philosophical Hermeneutics*; University of California Press, 1977, p. xiii; also Gadamer, implicitly in his essay "Philosophical Foundations," pp. 114–115, and by his characterization of Dilthey as a "historicist," p. 117). Rudolf Makkreel has shown that Dilthey sought to avoid an ontological break between nature and history by distinguishing the raw material of history—presumably what Bloch and Ricoeur mean by "traces"—from the subject matter. The former is provided by nature; it becomes historical when man stamps his impress on it, and it is methodologically interpreted: "Man knows abstractly that he is a part of nature, but he can intuitively understand his participation in the transformation of nature as it is objectified and preserved in the processes of his activity and understanding (Rudolf A. Makkreel, *Dilthey: Philosopher of the Human Studies;* Princeton Univer-

sity Press, 1975, pp. 306–307). Thus objectification is a function of the subject's interpretative process, not an independent entity over against the interpreting subject.

34. Ricoeur, *History and Truth,* p. 35.

35. W. Stark, Introduction to Max Scheler, *The Nature of Sympathy,* tr. by Peter Heath (Yale University Press, 1954), p. xxxi.

36. Scheler, *The Nature of Sympathy,* p. xi.

37. Makkreel, *Dilthey,* p. 308; Wilhelm Dilthey, *Gesammelte Schriften,* Vol. VII, p. 146.

38. E. E. Evans-Pritchard, *Social Anthropology and Other Essays* (Free Press of Glencoe, 1964), p. 173. He warns, however, against historicists who think they can account for cultural developments solely on the basis of antecedents; he would insist, rather, on the power and importance of the unique and unprecedented. One's attention must be given to both the typical and the novel features of historical phenomena (p. 175).

39. Ibid., pp. 174–175, 184–185, 186–187. Evans-Pritchard's point of view is affirmed by Lucy Mair in her widely used *An Introduction to Social Anthropology* (2d ed., Oxford: Clarendon Press, 1972), especially the parallels between ancient and contemporary preindustrial societies (p. 46). Concerning structuralist anthropology, which discusses all of reality in terms of structures of binary opposition, located ultimately in the human mind, she remarks in characteristic British understatement, "Other contemporary anthropologists thought sounder constructives might be built on less ambitious premises" (p. 51).

40. Alfred Schutz and Thomas Luckmann, *The Structures of the Life-World,* tr. by R. M. Zaner and H. T. Engelhardt, Jr. (Northwestern University Press, 1973); a more specific treatment of the question of religious knowledge (as opposed to magic, mysticism, and science) is offered by Judith Willer in *The Social Determination of Knowledge* (Prentice-Hall, 1971).

41. Schutz and Luckmann, *The Structures of the Life-World,* p. 250.

42. Ibid., p. 249.

43. Peter L. Berger, *The Sacred Canopy: Elements of a Sociological Theory of Religion* (Doubleday & Co., 1969).

44. Ibid., pp. 25–26.

45. Schutz and Luckmann, *The Structures of the Life-World,* pp. 7, 241.

46. H. Richard Niebuhr, *Christ and Culture* (Harper & Brothers, 1951).

47. Bryan R. Wilson, *Magic and the Millennium: A Sociological Study of Religious Movements of Protest Among Tribal and*

*Third-World Peoples* (Harper & Row, 1973).

48. Max Weber, *The Sociology of Religion;* Introduction by Talcott Parsons; tr. by Ephraim Fischoff from the 4th German ed. (Beacon Press, 1964). See further discussion in Chapter 3, note 1, below.

49. Weber, *The Sociology of Religion,* especially pp. 43–60.

50. Hans J. Mol, *Identity and the Sacred* (Free Press, Div. of Macmillan Publishing Co., 1977), pp. 45–46.

51. Ibid., pp. 12–14; on ritual, pp. 233–245; on myth, pp. 246–261.

52. Discussed by Northrop Frye in *Anatomy of Criticism* (Princeton University Press, 1957), pp. 86–87.

## 2. CONSTRUCTING THE COSMOS

1. Schutz and Luckmann, *The Structures of the Life-World,* p. 3.

2. Ibid., p. 4.

3. Ibid., p. 7.

4. Ibid., pp. 97–98.

5. Ibid., pp. 249–250.

6. Ibid., p. 284.

7. Ibid., p. 292.

8. Ibid., p. 285.

9. Ibid., p. 296; Berger (*The Sacred Canopy,* p. 191) acknowledges his debt to Schutz for the insight that "the sociologically most relevant knowledge" is precisely what is taken for granted —the "and-so-forth" idealization—rather than a concisely built up theoretical and theological knowledge system.

10. Ibid., p. 299.

11. On the factor of social and cultural adaptation, see Jean Piaget's *Structuralism,* discussed below, pp. 101–108.

12. Helmer Ringgren, *Word and Wisdom: Studies in the Hypostatization of Divine Qualities and Function in the Ancient Near East* (Lund: H. Ohlsson, 1947), pp. 45–49; "Maat . . . incorporates the cosmic order and the king, by virtue of his functioning in the ritual, upholds the universal rule." Also Gerhard von Rad, *Wisdom in Israel,* tr. by James D. Martin (Abingdon Press, 1972), p. 73.

13. James M. Reese, in *Hellenistic Influence on the Book of Wisdom and Its Consequences* (Rome: Biblical Institute Press, 1970), has demonstrated the extensive, word-for-word corre-

spondences between what "Solomon" says about wisdom and what Isis devotees say about her in preserved inscriptions and documents.

14. Reginald E. Witt, *Isis in the Graeco-Roman World* (Cornell University Press, 1971), p. 106.

15. Jacob Neusner, *From Politics to Piety: The Emergence of Pharisaic Judaism* (Prentice-Hall, 1973).

16. Hengel, *Judaism and Hellenism,* Vol. I, pp. 171ff. and notes.

17. Ibid., Vol. I, pp. 162–164.

18. Testament of Naphtali 3.3.

19. Cf. Berger, *The Sacred Canopy,* pp. 105–125.

20. Ibid., p. 107.

21. Conveniently summarized by M. Hengel, *Judaism and Hellenism,* Vol. I, pp. 58–78.

22. Berger, *The Sacred Canopy,* p. 107.

23. See, for example, Ernst Käsemann, "Paul and Early Catholicism," in *New Testament Questions of Today* (Fortress Press, 1969), pp. 236–238.

24. A professor of New Testament of a leading German Protestant faculty, a student of Bultmann, admitted to me that in his view, once the high point of Christianity was revealed in Paul's letter to the Romans, the entire subsequent history of the church runs downhill.

25. Mol, *Identity and the Sacred,* p. 15.

26. Ibid., p. 23.

27. Ibid., p. 23. Cf. Talcott Parsons, "Christianity and Modern Industrial Society," in Edward Tiryakian (ed.), *Sociological Theory, Values, and Sociocultural Change* (Free Press of Glencoe, 1963). Cited by Mol, *Identity and the Sacred,* p. 23.

28. Mol, *Identity and the Sacred,* p. 3. I find it somewhat confusing to use "identity" as a technical term in two different senses: the personal-psychological sense of group or individual identity and the ontological or classificatory sense of substantive continuity. The term is used in the present study in the former sense.

29. Arnold J. Toynbee, *A Study of History*, abridged ed. (Oxford University Press, 1947).

30. Gershom G. Scholem, *Major Trends in Jewish Mysticism,* 3d ed. (Schocken Books, 1961); also, *Jewish Gnosticism, Merkabah Mysticism and Talmudic Tradition* (Jewish Theological Seminary, 1960). See my discussion of this phenomenon in my *Jesus in History,* 2d ed. (Harcourt Brace Jovanovich, 1977), p. 235.

31. Scholem, *Major Trends in Jewish Mysticism.*

32. For a fuller discussion of Jesus as revealer in John and the nature of the mystical community, see my *Jesus in History* (1977), pp. 230–236.

33. Werner Jaeger, *Early Christianity and Greek Paideia* (Oxford University Press, 1962), has shown that it was not until the end of the fourth century that Christianity indeed became the public religion of the state. Even when the persecutions ceased, it could fulfill the unifying and consolidating function intended by Constantine only if it could (1) "overcome the conflict within its own ranks as to what was to be regarded as the authentic form of the Christian faith" and if it could (2) "prove itself capable of attracting the large and important percentage of the pagan population still opposed to it." This intellectual elite, whose influence was out of all proportion to their numbers, resisted Christianity on cultural rather than purely religious grounds, since they perceived a threat to *paideia,* itself regarded as a kind of religion, which had for centuries served as a unifying cultural ideology (pp. 70–72). Only when the Christian thinkers were able to synthesize that ideal with the Christian religion as a way of life in which the Platonic-Aristotelian ideal found its fulfillment did the intellectual hostility subside (p. 141, n. 9).

## 3. LEADERSHIP AND AUTHORITY

1. Max Weber, *The Sociology of Religion,* pp. 60ff. Cf. the assessment of Weber's thesis by Talcott Parsons in his Introduction, pp. xxxix–xlvii. See also Max Weber, in *Max Weber on Charisma and Institution Building,* ed. by S. N. Eisenstadt (University of Chicago Press, 1968), p. 253.

2. K. O. L. Burridge, *New Heaven, New Earth: A Study of Millenarian Activities* (Schocken Books, 1969).

3. Ibid., pp. 97–99.

4. T. Parsons, in his Introduction to Max Weber's *Sociology of Religion,* p. xliv.

5. Mol, *Identity and the Sacred,* p. 31.

6. Ibid., pp. 31–32.

7. Weber, *Sociology of Religion,* pp. 59, 139; *Max Weber on Charisma,* pp. 254–259.

8. Max Weber, "The Sociology of Charismatic Authority," in *From Max Weber,* tr. and ed. by H. H. Gerth and C. Wright Mills (Oxford University Press, 1958), pp. 245–246.

9. Mol, *Identity and the Sacred,* p. 45.

10. Ibid., p. 46.

11. Josephus, *Jewish War* II.408.

12. Josephus, in his *Jewish War*, refers to Simon (II.57), Athronges (II.60), and unnamed revolutionaries in II.72–76, 252–253.

13. Josephus, *Jewish War* II.254–256.

14. Ibid., II.257.

15. Ibid.

16. Lily Ross Taylor, *The Divinity of the Roman Emperor* (American Philological Association, 1931), pp. 113–114. For translation of the oracle from Virgil's Fourth Eclogue, see H. C. Kee, *Origins of Christianity*, pp. 113–114.

17. A brief sketch of the Sibylline tradition, with bibliography, is given in Edgar Hennecke, *New Testament Apocrypha*, Vol. II, ed. by Wilhelm Schneemelcher, tr. by R. McL. Wilson (Westminster Press, 1965). Article by A. Kurfess, "Christian Sibyllines," pp. 703–708.

18. Weber declared that if the charismatic leader wants to be recognized as a prophet, he must perform miracles. His power and recognition, and the devotion of his followers rests on his ability to demonstrate the extraordinary, to challenge tradition, and thereby to confirm his link with the divine. (Weber, "The Sociology of Charismatic Authority," p. 248.)

19. Rudolf Bultmann, *Theology of the New Testament*, Vol. I (Charles Scribner's Sons, 1955), pp. 130–131.

20. For summary and evidence, see my essay "Isis, Wisdom, and the Logos of John" in the forthcoming collection of essays from the Boston University Institute for Philosophy and Theology (1977–78), *Myth, Symbol, Reality*, ed. by Alan Olson, to be published by University of Notre Dame Press, 1980.

21. Ibid.

22. Origen, *Contra Celsum* I.69; I.6.

23. Cf. John M. Hull, *Hellenistic Magic and the Synoptic Tradition* (Alec R. Allenson, 1974). His broad definition of magic and his lack of interest in the possibility of different life worlds in this period preclude his making any distinction between miracle and magic. The same may be said of Morton Smith's *Jesus the Magician* (Harper & Row, 1978). A. D. Nock was also unwilling to make a sharp differentiation.

24. Bronislaw Malinowski, *Magic, Science and Religion* (1925; Doubleday & Co., Anchor Books, 1954).

25. Ibid., p. 90.

26. Ibid., pp. 88–89.

27. Ibid., p. 24.

28. Ibid., p. 48.

29. Marcel Mauss, *A General Theory of Magic,* tr. by Robert Brain (W. W. Norton & Co., 1972), p. 136.

30. Lucy Mair, *An Introduction to Social Anthropology,* 2d ed., pp. 225–229.

31. Ibid., pp. 232–237. E. E. Evans-Pritchard, however, in *Nuer Religion* (Oxford: Clarendon Press, 1956), shows how these factors are difficult to differentiate in some religions in which objects associated with magic rites, such as leeches, are regarded as incarnating divine spirits (p. 95).

32. Judith Willer, *The Social Determination of Knowledge,* pp. 15, 29.

33. John Ferguson, *The Religions of the Roman Empire* (Cornell University Press, 1970), p. 159.

34. Gerardus van der Leeuw, *Religion in Essence and Manifestation* (London: Allen & Unwin, 1938), p. 568. Cf. J. Gwyn Griffiths (tr. and ed.), *The Isis-Book (Metamorphoses, Book XI)* (Leiden: E. J. Brill, 1976), p. 50. In his illuminating study of Apuleius' "Isis Book," Griffiths quotes approvingly Van der Leeuw's description of the sign-character of miracle, but then goes on to blur the distinction from magic by differentiating a higher type of magic (i.e., miracle) from a lower type, which is dependent on formulas and technique. He notes, however, that for Apuleius the greatest miracle is his own spiritual regeneration, symbolized by his transformation from ass to human. One might add that this miracle is described as being accomplished in response to the petition addressed to the deity, not by ritual or thaumaturgic performance. It is miracle, not magic.

35. Peter Brown, "Sorcery, Demons and the Rise of Christianity," in his *Religion and Society in the Age of Saint Augustine.*

36. Dodds, *Pagan and Christian in an Age of Anxiety,* p. 124, n. 1.

37. Ibid., p. 125.

38. Judith Willer, *The Social Determination of Knowledge,* p. 83.

39. Martin Hengel, *Nachfolge und Charisma (Beihefte zur Zeitschrift für die neutestamentliche Wissenschaft,* Vol. 34 (Berlin: Töpelmann, 1968), p. 59. Cf. *Max Weber on Charisma,* p. 255.

40. Gerd Theissen, "Itinerant Radicals: Sociology of Literature Aspects of the Tradition of the Words of Jesus in Early Christianity," *Radical Religion,* Vol. 2 (Berkeley, 1975), pp. 84–93.

41. Hengel, *Nachfolge und Charisma,* p. 37. Cf. *Max Weber on Charisma,* pp. 21, 59.

42. Plutarch reports that Alexander came and stood by the tub

in which Diogenes was sunning himself, and then identified himself as Alexander. When Alexander asked if he could do anything for Diogenes, the crusty Cynic replied that he could move aside and stop blocking the light.

43. Ramsay MacMullen, *Enemies of the Roman Order,* p. 59.

44. Pliny the Younger, Letter to Trajan, *Letters* X.xcvi; Trajan's Response, ibid., X.xcvii.

45. Detailed in MacMullen, *Enemies of the Roman Order,* pp. 61–70.

46. Ibid., pp. 128–162.

47. *Max Weber on Charisma,* pp. 254–255. Charismatic authentication is by "special magical *(sic)* or ecstatic abilities."

## 4. PERSONAL AND SOCIAL IDENTITY IN THE NEW COMMUNITY

1. Arthur Darby Nock, *Conversion: The Old and the New in Religion from Alexander the Great to Augustine of Hippo* (Oxford University Press, 1933), p. 7.

2. Ibid.

3. Mol, *Identity and the Sacred,* p. 50.

4. Ibid.

5. Ibid., pp. 52–53.

6. Nock, *Conversion,* p. 7.

7. Sections I–III of the Damascus Document, excerpted from Millar Burrows, *The Dead Sea Scrolls* (Viking Press, 1955).

8. Translating *hoi par' autou* as "family," not "friends." Cf. Mark 3:31ff., where those waiting outside are Jesus' mother and brothers and sisters.

9. Mol, *Identity and the Sacred,* p. 53.

10. Ibid. A noticeable change in outward bearing and inner attitude is attested by Lucian in his description of his encounter with Nigrinus the Platonic philosopher (Lucian, *Wisdom of Nigrinus;* Loeb Classical Library, Lucian, Vol. I).

11. A. J. Festugière, *Epicurus and His Gods,* tr. by C. W. Chilton (1956; Russell and Russell, 1969), p. 39.

12. Ibid. The classic studies of conversion by William James in *The Varieties of Religious Experience* (1902; repr. Modern Library, n.d.), pp. 186–253, describe the phenomenon solely in terms of the individual's experience, and leave out of account conversion as a ground of group identity.

13. Quoted by Mol, *Identity and the Sacred,* p. 51, from Arthur Koestler, *The God That Failed* (London: Hamish Hamilton, 1951), p. 32.

14. E. Bigone, *L'Aristotele Perduto e la Formazione filosofica di Epicuro* (Florence, 1936), Vol. I, p. 109. Quoted by Benjamin Farrington, *The Faith of Epicurus* (London: George Weidenfeld & Nicholson, 1967), p. 104.

15. Farrington, *The Faith of Epicurus*, p. 103.

16. Festugière, *Epicurus and His Gods*, pp. 28, 33, 35, 42.

17. N. D. Fustel de Coulanges, *The Ancient City: A Classic Study of the Religious and Civil Institutions of Ancient Greece and Rome* (repr. of 1864 ed., Doubleday & Co., 1955), p. 86.

18. Ibid., p. 319.

19. Nock, *Conversion*, p. 29; later (third to fifth centuries) the Gnostics did develop conventicles but they were an excrescence on Christianity.

20. Juvenal, *Satire* 6, lines 540–541, 512–516; quoted from Jérôme Carcopino, *Daily Life in Ancient Rome*, tr. by E. O. Lorimer (Yale University Press [1940], 1977).

21. Lily Ross Taylor, *The Cults of Ostia* (repr. of 1913 ed., Ares Publications, 1976), pp. 68, 83.

22. Ibid., p. 95.

23. Ibid.

24. Carcopino, *Daily Life in Ancient Rome*, p. 129.

25. Nock, *Conversion*, pp. 80–88.

26. Lucian, *Alexander*. See analysis by Nock, *Conversion*, pp. 91–96.

27. Pliny the Younger, Letter to Trajan, *Letters* X.xcvi; Trajan's response, ibid., X.xcvii.

28. Origen, *Contra Celsum* I.2.1; III.55.19.

29. The excavators of Corinth found a crudely carved stone lintel with an inscription in Greek, probably from the first century, and which almost certainly read: "(Syna)gogue of the Hebr-(ews)." It apparently had been placed over the door of one of the small rectangular shops lining the street that sloped down from the central forum of the city to the port. Acts 18:7 notes that the nascent church in Corinth assembled in the house of Titius Justus, a man who lived next to the synagogue.

30. While there are reports of the dead being summoned up from the grave, as in the appearance of Samuel's ghost (I Sam. 28), only in Dan. 12:2–3 do we have indications of a belief in bodily resurrection.

31. Earliest attestation in Apollonius of Rhodes, mid-third century B.C.

32. Older but useful summary of evidence by K. Lake in *The Beginnings of Christianity*, Vol. V, pp. 74–96.

33. Discussion and references in Fustel de Coulanges, *The*

*Ancient City,* pp. 30, 92–95. For a brief summary of attitudes toward women in the Roman world and in the New Testament writings, see Evelyn and Frank Stagg, *Woman in the World of Jesus* (Westminster Press, 1978).

34. The senate's inability to censure women is reported by Livy, and the declaration that the husband is the sole judge of the wife is from Cato. References in Fustel de Coulanges, *The Ancient City.*

35. Theissen, *Sociology of Early Palestinian Christianity.*

36. Ibid., p. 7.

37. Ibid., p. 15.

38. Gerd Theissen, "Wanderradikalismus, Literatursoziologische Aspekte der Überlieferung von Worten Jesu im Urchristentum," *Zeitschrift für Theologie und Kirche,* Vol. 70 (1973), p. 254; Eng. tr. by A. Wire, in *Radical Religion,* Vol. 2 (Berkeley, 1975). Ernst Käsemann has advanced the proposal that the apodictic sayings of Jesus, especially those of the formulaic type ("if any . . ."; "Whoever . . ., he shall"), originated with Christian prophets and simply claim the authority of Jesus and his mission ("for my sake and the gospel's"). See "Sentences of Holy Law," in Ernst Käsemann, *New Testament Questions of Today* (Fortress Press, 1969), pp. 66–81.

39. The issue of the authorship of Colossians, including its use of the *Haustafel,* is discussed by Werner Georg Kümmel, *Introduction to the New Testament,* tr. by H. C. Kee, rev. ed. (Abingdon Press, 1975), pp. 340–346; Kümmel concludes that Paul wrote this letter.

40. Gerd Theissen, "Soziale Schichtung in der korinthischer Gemeinde," ZThK, Vol. 65 (1974), p. 235.

41. Gerd Theissen, "Legitimation und Lebensunterhalt: Ein Beitrag zur Soziologie urchristlicher Missionäre," *New Testament Studies,* Vol. 21 (1975), pp. 192–221.

42. Dio Cassius (LXVII.14.2) identifies the relatives of Domitian executed by his order as atheists who had wandered into Jewish practices. That could mean that they had converted to Judaism or at least were sympathetic toward Judaism (thus Michael Grant, in *The Jews in the Roman World;* Charles Scribner's Sons, 1973, p. 225) or that they converted to a religion the Romans could have regarded as a Jewish sect, i.e., Christianity. The arguments and the archaeological evidence for the latter interpretation are conveniently summarized by F. F. Bruce, *New Testament History* (Doubleday & Co., Anchor Book, 1971), pp. 413–414.

## 5. CULT AND CULTURE

1. Apuleius, *Metamorphoses* XI.4-5.
2. Cf. H. J. Cadbury in Foakes-Jackson et al., *The Beginnings of Christianity,* Vol. IV, pp. 250–252; also L. R. Taylor, "Artemis of Ephesus," ibid., Vol. V, pp. 251–256.
3. Mol, *Identity and the Sacred,* pp. 11–14.
4. Jean Piaget, *Structuralism,* tr. and ed. by Chaninah Maschler (Harper & Row, 1971).
5. Cf. Claude Lévi-Strauss, *The Raw and the Cooked* [1964], tr. by John and Doreen Weightman (Harper & Row, 1969). In his *Structural Anthropology* [1958], tr. by Claire Jacobson and Brooke Grundfest Schoepf (Doubleday & Co., 1967), Lévi-Strauss asserts that "it is not comparison that supports generalization but the other way around." The mind unconsciously imposes forms on the content; they are not arrived at inductively.
6. In *The Savage Mind* (University of Chicago Press, 1967), Lévi-Strauss declares that the changes brought about by history do not affect the human mind itself. While history is useful for classifying information, it belongs to the past: "History leads to everything, but on condition that it be left behind" (p. 262).
7. See note 5 above.
8. K. O. L. Burridge, "Lévi-Strauss and Myth," in Edmund Leach (ed.), *The Structural Study of Myth and Totemism* (Barnes & Noble, 1967), p. 113. Clifford Geertz, in *The Interpretation of Cultures* (Basic Books, 1973), offers an extended analysis and devastating critique of Lévi-Strauss (pp. 345–359), in which he raises the question whether Lévi-Strauss's disillusionment with the romantic view of the "noble savage" he set out to study, as reflected in *Tristes Tropiques* (1955; tr. by John and Doreen Weightman; Atheneum Press, 1974), has not led him to transmute that "romantic passion . . . into the hypermodern intellectualism of retreating from the harsh realities of observable data in primitive culture to the verdant fields of intellectual speculation and aesthetic gratification." Commenting on *The Savage Mind* Geertz asks: "Is this transformation science or alchemy? . . . Is this very 'simple transformation' which produced a general theory out of a personal disappointment real or a sleight of hand? Is it a genuine demolition of the walls which seem to separate mind from mind by showing that the walls are surface structures only, or is it an elaborately disguised evasion necessitated by a failure to breach them when they are directly encountered?" Lévi-Strauss wondered in *Tristes Tropiques* if the attraction to savages was not the consequence of himself possessing a "neo-

lithic" mind. Geertz responds with a question, "Is he, like some uprooted neolithic intelligence cast away on a reservation, shuffling the debris of old traditions in a vain attempt to revivify a primitive faith whose moral beauty is still apparent, but from which relevance and credibility have long since departed?" (p. 359).

9. Daniel Patte, *What Is Structural Exegesis?* (Fortress Press, 1976); also Dan O. Via, Jr., *Kerygma and Comedy in the New Testament* (Fortress Press, 1975); F. Bovon (ed.), *Analyse Structurale et Exégèse Biblique* (Neuchâtel, 1971); Bruno de Solages, *Comment sont nés les évangiles?* (Toulouse [Privat], 1973).

10. J. Starobinski, "Le Démoniaque de Gerasa: Analyse littéraire de Marc 5:1–20," in Bovon (ed.), *Analyse Structurale et Exégèse Biblique*, pp. 63–94.

11. Ibid., p. 64.

12. Ibid., p. 72.

13. Ibid., p. 78.

14. Jean Piaget, *Structuralism*.

15. Ibid., pp. 5–7.

16. Ibid., p. 35.

17. Ibid., p. 14.

18. Ibid., p. 50.

19. Ibid., pp. 71–72. Piaget carefully distinguishes what he here calls the "epistemic self" from the individual or isolated ego. See also p. 139.

20. Lévi-Strauss, *Structural Anthropology,* p. 21.

21. Piaget, *Structuralism,* p. 114: "We must admit that we do not really understand why the mind is more truly honored when turned into a collection of permanent schemata than when it is viewed as the yet unfinished product of continual self-construction."

22. Ibid., p. 118.

23. Ibid., p. 127, with reference to Godelier's article, "Système, structure, et contradiction dans le Capital," in *Les Temps Modernes* (1966), p. 857, n. 55.

24. Samuel Sandmel, "Parallelomania," *Journal of Biblical Literature,* Vol. 81 (1962), pp. 1–13.

25. Mol, *Identity and the Sacred,* p. 246.

26. G. S. Kirk, *Myth: Its Meaning and Functions in Ancient and Other Cultures* (University of California Press, 1970). See further on myth: Mircea Eliade, "The Morphology and Function of Myths," in *Patterns in Comparative Religion,* tr. by Rosemary Sheed (Meridian Books, 1963), pp. 410–434, and compact bibliography on pp. 435–436, where a range of approaches to myth

(historical, anthropological, psychological) is offered.

27. See my forthcoming essay, "Isis, Wisdom, and the Logos of John" (referred to in Chapter 3, note 20, above); see also Chapter 3, note 17, above.

28. For example, only the Gospel of the Nazarenes and the Gospel of the Ebionites are concerned with Jesus' career. The Gospel of Peter and the Acts of Pilate expand on the passion narrative, and the infancy gospels (Protevangelium of James; Infancy Gospel of Thomas) heighten the miraculous aspects of his childhood. But many of the rest—the gospels of Thomas, of the Hebrews, of the Egyptians, of Truth, and of Mary, and the Apocryphon of James—consist almost solely of revelatory utterances.

29. Gerhard von Rad, *Wisdom in Israel,* tr. by James D. Martin (Abingdon Press, 1972), pp. 263–283.

30. Otto Plöger, *Theocracy and Eschatology,* tr. by S. Rudman (John Knox Press, 1968), p. 50.

31. See my *Community of the New Age;* also *Jesus in History* (1977), pp. 111–119.

32. Kee, *Jesus in History* (1977), pp. 92–98, 111–117; *Community of the New Age,* pp. 117–119.

33. Wayne A. Meeks, *The Prophet-King: Moses Traditions and the Johannine Christology* (Supplement to *Novum Testamentum* XIV; Leiden: E. J. Brill, 1967).

34. Piaget, *Structuralism,* pp. 127–128.

35. Summarized in Marcel Simon, *Hercule et le Christianisme* (Paris, 1955), p. 63.

36. Kee, *Community of the New Age,* pp. 23–29, 84–85.

37. Transcriptions of aretalogies include Emma J. and Ludwig Edelstein, *Asclepius: A Collection and Interpretation of the Testimonies* (2 vols., Johns Hopkins Press, 1945–1946); R. Merkelbach, "Zwei Texte aus dem Sarapeum zu Thessalonike," *Zeitschrift für Papyrologie und Épigraphie,* Vol. 10 (1973), pp. 45–54; Yves Grandjean, *Une Nouvelle Aretalogie d'Isis à Maronée* (Leiden: E. J. Brill, 1975). Oration XLIX of Aelius Aristides is in praise of Sarapis *and* Asclepius. Sarapis made an incision in Aristides' head and relieved him of his ailment. He goes on to describe the incorporeal transport of the soul by mystic ladders.

38. Thus Plutarch, *Lives,* "Nicias," 23.

39. David L. Tiede, *The Charismatic Figure as Miracle Worker,* Society of Biblical Literature Dissertations Series, No. 1 (Scholars Press, 1972), pp. 41, 51.

40. Attested by such skeptical ancient writers as Celsus (second century) and Lucian of Samosata (b. ca. 125, d. after 180) as well as by Origen in his reply to Celsus (e.g., *Contra Celsum* 1.60).

Recent historians have noted the widespread belief in magic and sorcery: see Peter Brown, "Sorcery, Demons and the Rise of Christianity," *Religion and Society in the Age of Saint Augustine,* pp. 119–146; Dodds, *Pagan and Christian in an Age of Anxiety,* pp. 123–125; Gerd Theissen, *Urchristliche Wundergeschichten* (Gütersloh: Gerd Mohn, 1974), pp. 264–271.

41. Tiede, *The Charismatic Figure,* p. 61.

42. Carl Holladay, *Theios Aner in Hellenistic Judaism,* Society of Biblical Literature Dissertations Series, No. 40 (Scholars Press, 1977), p. 195.

43. Theissen, *Urchristliche Wundergeschichten,* p. 42.

44. Ibid.

45. Already in the Gospel of John, the miracles are called "signs" (John 2:3; 4:54; 20:30–31), with the implication that their symbolic value has largely eclipsed their evidential functions. That impression is confirmed by the way in which John shifts from recounting the signs to discoursing on their inner meaning.

46. E.g., IV Macc. 6:24–29.

47. Cf. note 26 above.

48. Mol, *Identity and the Sacred,* p. 233.

49. Acts 18:24 to 19:6, which separates water baptism from Spirit baptism, is unusual in the New Testament and, if historically based, probably reflects the difficulties some may have had in differentiating the eschatological sects that grew around the figures of John and Jesus, respectively. Or it may be, as Ernst Haenchen suggests (*The Acts of the Apostles,* Westminster Press, 1971, pp. 554–557), a Lukan device to demonstrate Apollos' dependence on apostolic instruction and approval.

50. Bultmann thinks John is eliminating the Sacraments, replacing them by purely spiritual participation (*The Gospel of John;* Westminster Press, 1971).

51. Text in Theodor H. Gaster, *The Dead Sea Scriptures* (Doubleday & Co., 1956), p. 310. Discussion in Kee, *Jesus in History,* 2d ed., pp. 66–71, on the relationship of Eucharist to Passover and eschatological meal, with bibliography. On the details of the church as eschatological community, especially in Mark, see my *Community of the New Age,* pp. 107–116.

52. Ignatius, *Epistle to the Trallians* 2.

53. Justin Martyr, *Apology* I. Relief representations of the Mithraic cult show a common cup and circular wafers marked with a cross.

54. Ignatius, *Epistle to the Smyrnaeans* 9.

55. Baptism as enlightenment is treated at length by Justin Martyr, *Apol.* I.61 and by Clement of Alexandria, *Paed.* I.6.

Clement describes the process of sanctification as launched with baptism: "Being baptized, we are illuminated, we become sons; being made sons, we are made perfect (mature); being made perfect, we are made immortal."

56. Plutarch, *Moralia* 20.

57. Max Weber noted that religions shift from the social stratum in which they arose to another in which they flourish, as Christianity moved from a context of rural itinerancy to one of urban stability (in "Social Psychology of the World Religions," *From Max Weber*, p. 269).

58. See my discussion of "The Historical Links of the Markan Community with First-Century Judaism," in *Community of the New Age*, pp. 97–100.

59. Nils Alstrup Dahl, *The Crucified Messiah* (Augsburg Publishing House, 1974), pp. 23f. Cf. M. Hengel, *Was Jesus a Revolutionist?* (Fortress Press, 1971), p. 15.

60. *Reimarus: Fragments of a Life of Jesus,* Eng. tr. by R. S. Fraser, ed. by Charles Talbert (Fortress Press, 1970).

61. Karl Kautsky, *Foundations of Christianity,* tr. by Henry F. Mins (1925; S. A. Russell, 1953).

62. S. G. F. Brandon, *Jesus and the Zealots* (Charles Scribner's Sons, 1968). This position is also set forth in popular works such as Joel Carmichael, *The Death of Jesus* (The Macmillan Co., 1963), and Hugh J. Schonfield, *The Passover Plot* (London: Hutchinson & Co., 1965).

63. Martin Hengel, *Die Zeloten, Untersuchungen zur Freiheitsbewegung in der Zeit von Herodes I bis 70 n. Chr.* (Leiden: E. J. Brill, 1961).

64. Hengel, *Was Jesus a Revolutionist?* pp. 20–29.

65. Ibid., p. 19.

66. Ibid., p. 12, n. 39.

67. For the time and circumstances of the writing of The Book of Revelation, see Kümmel, *Introduction to the New Testament,* (1975), pp. 446–469.


## 6. SOCIAL FUNCTIONS
## OF THE NEW TESTAMENT WRITINGS

1. René Wellek and Austin Warren, *Theory of Literature,* rev. ed. (Harcourt, Brace & Co., 1956).

2. Ibid., p. 34.

3. Ibid., p. 65.

4. Ibid., p. 66.

5. Ibid., p. 93.

6. Ibid., p. 101.

7. Ibid., p. 104.

8. Ibid., p. 105.

9. Ibid., p. 102.

10. Ibid., p. 158.

11. Ibid., p. 235. This recalls, of course, Piaget's transformation of structures. (See Chapter 5 above.)

12. Ibid., p. 245.

13. Proposals to date the Gospels before A.D. 50 rest on a blend of wishful thinking and scholarly games, as in John A. T. Robinson, *Redating the New Testament* (Westminster Press, 1976).

14. For representative letters of this sort see my *The Origins of Christianity: Sources and Documents* (Prentice-Hall, 1973), pp. 262–265.

15. See the older but still useful discussion of the Letter of Aristeas by H. T. Andrews in R. H. Charles, *Apocrypha and Pseudepigrapha*, Vol. II (Oxford: Clarendon Press, 1913), pp. 83–93. See also the recent and general study by William G. Doty, *Letters in Primitive Christianity* (Fortress Press, 1973).

16. Only in Galatians and II Thessalonians does Paul fail to speak of his fellow Christians as "beloved."

17. The international leader of the opposition to the Two-Document Hypothesis (priority of Mark's Gospel; a written source common to Luke and Matthew) is W. R. Farmer. Like his ally Hans-Herbert Stoldt, in *Geschichte und Kritik der Markus-Hypothese* (Göttingen: Vandenhoeck & Ruprecht, 1977), he can point to the use of these theories for logically fallacious ends, such as attempting to prove the historicity of the Markan account on the grounds of Markan priority. But Stoldt takes refuge in the fantasyland of an Ur-Markus Hypothesis (for which the evidence cannot be proved or discounted, since it does not exist). And Farmer has never been able to make a conceptually and linguistically convincing case that Mark is dependent on either Matthew or Luke. R. Morgenthaler's statistical approach, and his interpretation of the evidence, make an as yet impregnable base for Markan priority (*Statistische Synopse;* Stuttgart and Zurich, 1971). For the plausibility of the Q hypothesis and the probable extent of Q see Kee, *Jesus in History* (1977).

18. Erhardt Güttgemanns, *Offene Fragen zur Formgeschichte des Evangeliums.* See Chapter 1, note 13 above. On orality, see Walter J. Ong, *Interfaces of the Word* (Cornell University Press, 1977).

19. The first form has been identified by Richard A. Edwards as an "eschatological correlative" to designate four sections in Q:

Luke 11:30; 17:24, 26, 28–30 (*A Theology of Q;* Fortress Press, 1976). The second formula has been called "Sentences of Holy Law," by Ernst Käsemann in *New Testament Questions for Today,* pp. 66–81, but a more appropriate title might be simply "eschatological pronouncements."

20. For a detailed treatment of Q as an eschatological document, see Kee, *Jesus in History* (1977), pp. 87–119, and Edwards, *A Theology of Q.*

21. The provenance of Mark is discussed more fully in my *Community of the New Age* (Westminster Press, 1977), pp. 77–105, esp. pp. 97–105.

22. Gerd Theissen, "Itinerant Radicals: Sociology of Literature Aspects of the Tradition of the Words of Jesus in Early Christianity," *Radical Religion,* Vol. 2 (Berkeley, 1975), pp. 84–93.

23. For a detailed discussion of the sociological process and consequences of "disconfirmation" of millenarian expectations, including those of the early Christian movement and various Jewish and Christian sects, see Leon Festinger et al., *When Prophecy Fails* (University of Minnesota Press, 1956).

24. See my "The Function of Scriptural Quotations and Allusions in Mark 11–16," in *Jesus und Paulus,* ed. by E. E. Ellis and E. Grässer (Göttingen: Vandenhoeck & Ruprecht, 1975), pp. 165–188.

25. This structure of Matthew has been challenged by J. D. Kingsbury, *Matthew: Structure, Christology, Kingdom* (Fortress Press, 1975).

26. See the analysis by Günther Bornkamm in G. Bornkamm et al., *Tradition and Interpretation in Matthew,* tr. by Percy Scott (Westminster Press, 1963); also Wolfgang Trilling, *Das wahre Israel* (Leipzig: St. Benno Verlag, 1959). For a fuller statement of the interpretation of Matthew offered here, see my *Jesus in History* (1977), pp. 165–185, with bibliography.

27. D. R. Stuart, *Epochs of Greek and Roman Biography* (University of California Press, 1928), p. 250.

28. Ibid., p. 251.

29. Charles H. Talbert, *What Is a Gospel? The Genre of the Canonical Gospels* (Fortress Press, 1977).

30. Ibid., p. 79.

31. Ibid. On birth, p. 28; on ascension and absence of physical body, p. 27; on benefactions as ground of immortality, p. 36.

32. Ibid., pp. 41, 107, 109.

33. Ibid., p. 107. Mark has no birth or childhood stories, no tracing of ancestry, no ascension account (only a reported rising from the dead and a promised appearance, Mark 16:8), no suc-

cession narrative (only befuddled disciples).

34. Ben E. Perry, *The Ancient Romances: A Literary-Historical Account of Their Origins* (University of California Press, 1967), p. 10.

35. Ibid., pp. 345–346, 350, for a discussion of dates of the romances.

36. Talbert, *What Is a Gospel?* p. 101.

37. Talbert is able to dismiss the eschatological factor in Bultmann's argument differentiating Gospel from biography because eschatology is defined too narrowly: "With Christ world history had reached its end." It would be more accurate to say that, for Mark, with Christ the new age was about to begin, and the new covenant people were already in existence. See on this my *Community of the New Age,* esp. pp. 162–175.

38. E. Plumacher, *Lukas als hellenistische Schriftsteller* (Göttingen: Vandenhoeck & Ruprecht, 1972), has shown how closely Luke has followed standard literary techniques in the speeches and dramatic narratives in Acts as a way of portraying the heroes of the recent past (1) in the role of spokesmen for the goals and values of the community; and (2) as the courageous, wise leaders in the midst of crises in the primordial time of the movement.

39. On the romance as a middle-class phenomenon, with its mingling of morality and sentiment, see Perry, *The Ancient Romances,* pp. 72–74. The linking of historical or presumably historical characters with a mythical framework is an essential ingredient of the romance, especially since it contributes to moral and spiritual welfare, p. 77. On the theme of propaganda in the early church, see *Aspects of Religious Propaganda in Judaism and Early Christianity,* ed. by Elisabeth Schüssler Fiorenza (University of Notre Dame Press, 1976), and especially the introductory essay by the editor.

40. See the details of literary sophistication in Kümmel, *Introduction to the New Testament,* p. 411.

41. See A. Oepke, art. *"ekstasis,"* in G. Kittel and G. Friedrich (eds.), *Theological Dictionary of the New Testament,* tr. by Geoffrey W. Bromiley, Vol. II (Wm. B. Eerdmans Publishing Co., 1964), pp. 449–460. On Jewish apocalyptic, see Paul D. Hanson, *The Dawn of Apocalyptic* (Fortress Press, 1975); Otto Plöger, *Theocracy and Eschatology.*

42. Gershom G. Scholem, *Major Trends in Jewish Mysticism,* 3d ed. (Schocken Books, 1961).

43. Hengel, *Judaism and Hellenism,* Vol. I, p. 217. See also Günther Bornkamm, art. *"mystērion,"* in Kittel and Friedrich

(eds.), *Theological Dictionary of the New Testament,* Vol. III (1967), pp. 815–816.

44. Hengel, *Judaism and Hellenism,* Vol. I, pp. 207–208.

45. Ibid., p. 208.

46. Scholem, *Major Trends in Jewish Mysticism,* p. 9.

47. Ibid., p. 20. Quotations are from C. A. Bennett, *A Philosophical Study of Mysticism* (Yale University Press, 1931), p. 31.

48. Scholem, *Major Trends in Jewish Mysticism,* p. 9.

49. Ibid., p. 21.

50. Ibid., p. 27.

51. Ibid.

52. Scholem, *Jewish Gnosticism, Merkabah Mysticism and Talmudic Tradition,* p. 23: The "Apocalypse of Abraham more closely resembles a Merkabah text than any other in Jewish apocalyptic literature."

53. Jonas Greenfield, introduction to reprint of Hugo Odeberg (ed. and tr.), *3 Enoch; or, The Hebrew Book of Enoch* (1928 ed.; repr. KTAV Publishing House, 1973), p. xxvi. The document is perceived as descriptions of the Chariot-throne of Yahweh, and the heavenly ascent of Enoch to behold it. According to Scholem, *Jewish Gnosticism,* p. 50, in III Enoch the human being (Michael, Yahoel = Metatron) is identified with the transfigured Enoch.

54. Cf. my essay, "Satan, Magic, and Salvation in the Testament of Job," Society of Biblical Literature Seminar Papers, Vol. I (Scholars Press, 1974).

55. John Strugnell, "The Angelic Liturgy at Qumran," *Vetus Testamentum,* Supplement VII (Leiden: E. J. Brill, 1960), 318–345.

56. Nock, *Conversion,* pp. 26–31.

57. W. K. C. Guthrie, *Orpheus and Greek Religion,* rev. ed. (W. W. Norton & Co., 1966), esp. pp. 249ff.

58. Ibid., pp. 186–187.

59. Aristides, *Oratio* XLIX. 46–48; in Edelstein, *Asclepius: Testimonies.*

60. Diodorus Siculus, *Library of History,* Loeb Classical Library (Harvard University Press).

61. Walter A. Jayne, *The Healing Gods of Ancient Civilization* (1925; repr. AMS Press, 1976), p. 238.

62. Ibid., pp. 274ff. Aristides' cure from his complicated ailments through the beneficence of Asclepius and his subsequent religious experiences, including epiphanies of Asclepius, are recounted in Aristides' *Sacred Discourses;* these are reproduced in

summary form (with translated excerpts) by A. J. Festugière, in *Personal Religion Among the Greeks* (University of California Press, 1960), pp. 85–104.

63. A recently published aretalogy of Sarapis: R. Merkelbach, "Zwei Texte aus dem Sarapeum zu Thessalonike," *Zeitschrift für Papyrologie und Epigraphik,* Vol. 10 (1973), pp. 45–54; a newly available Isis aretalogy: in Grandjean, *Une nouvelle Aretalogie d'Isis à Maronée.*

64. For detailed evidence, see Edelstein, *Asclepius: Testimonies,* Vol. II: complete records from inscriptions, literature, and papyri.

65. The narrative also recalls features of the cult; cf. Reinhold Merkelbach, *Roman und Mysterium in der Antike* (Munich: C. H. Beck, 1962), pp. 91–113. See also Witt, *Isis in the Graeco-Roman World,* esp. pp. 241–254.

66. Apuleius, *Metamorphoses,* tr. by W. Adlington, Loeb Classical Library (Harvard University Press).

67. See my discussion in *Community of the New Age,* pp. 132–133.

68. The link between Paul's experience and Merkabah mysticism is recognized by Gershom Scholem, in *Jewish Gnosticism,* p. 17: Paul's ascension would have been familiar to his readers, "a Jewish conception that he, as well as his readers in Corinth, had brought over into the new Christian community."

69. Reading with p[66] and the corrector of Codex Sinaiticus, "divine one" is used instead of "only God," in order to differentiate Revealed and Revealer, and to bring out the apologetic intention: Jesus may resemble other divine revealers, but he is unique.

70. The links between Isis and Wisdom are set forth by James M. Reese (with reference to The Wisdom of Solomon) in *Hellenistic Influence on the Book of Wisdom and Its Consequences,* pp. 46–49. Also see Burton L. Mack, *Logos und Sophia: Untersuchungen zur Weisheitstheologie im hellenistischen Judentum* (Göttingen: Vandenhoeck & Ruprecht, 1973), pp. 90–95. Similar praises for the rule of Athena as agent of creation and divine revealer are offered in Aristides, *Oratio* II, although the element of personal benefaction is missing. W. L. Knox notes the resemblance between Jesus' word to God, "Glorify thy Son that thy Son also may glorify thee" (John 17:1) and a petition addressed to Isis in the magical papyri (Karl Preisendanz [ed.], *Papyri Graecae magicae* 7.503ff ): "Glorify me as I glorified the name of your son, Horus" (*Some Hellenistic Elements in Primitive Christianity;* London: British Academy, 1944; p. 85).

71. See the insightful study by Wayne A. Meeks, "The Man from Heaven in Johannine Sectarianism," *Journal of Biblical Literature,* Vol. 91 (1972), pp. 52–65.

72. Raymond E. Brown, *The Community of the Beloved Disciple* (Paulist Press, 1979).

73. R. P. C. Hanson, *Allegory and Event: A Study of the Sources and Significance of Origen's Interpretation of Scripture* (John Knox Press, 1959); Harry A. Wolfson, *The Philosophy of the Church Fathers,* Vol. I (Harvard University Press, 1956), pp. 24–72.

74. Origen, *Commentary on John* I.9–10.

75. Origen developed his own Christian Ennead, as his younger pagan contemporary Plotinus was to do in his Neoplatonic system.

76. Quoted by Eusebius, *Ecclesiastical History* III.39.3.

77. Summarized by Kümmel, *Introduction to the New Testament,* pp. 495–496.

78. Eusebius makes optional including it among the commonly accepted books, but he also makes optional including it among the disputed books (*Ecclesiastical History* III.25; II.23–24).

79. Convenient summaries with bibliography will be found in W. G. Kümmel, *Introduction to the New Testament,* pp. 475–510; Hennecke-Schneemelcher-Wilson, *New Testament Apocrypha,* Vol. I, pp. 21–59.

# Note to the British Edition

Books referred to in the notes have been published in British editions as follows:

Ian G. Barbour, *Myths, Models and Paradigms*, SCM Press 1974

Günther Bornkamm, Gerhard Barth and H. J. Held, *Tradition and Interpretation in Matthew*, SCM Press 1963

S. G. F. Brandon, *Jesus and the Zealots*, Manchester University Press 1967

Peter Brown, *Religion and Society in the Age of St Augustine*, Faber 1972

F. F. Bruce, *New Testament History*, Oliphants ²1971

Rudolf Bultmann, *The Gospel of John*, Blackwell 1971

—, *The History of the Synoptic Tradition*, Blackwell ²1968

—, *Jesus and the Word*, Fontana Books 1958

—, *Primitive Christianity in its Contemporary Setting*, Thames and Hudson 1956

—, *Theology of the New Testament* (two vols.), SCM Press 1952, 1955

K. O. L. Burridge, *New Heaven: New Earth*, Blackwell 1969

Millar Burrows, *The Dead Sea Scrolls*, Secker and Warburg 1956

H. J. Cadbury, *The Making of Luke-Acts*, SPCK 1924

Joel Carmichael, *The Death of Jesus*, Gollancz 1963

Norman Cohn, *The Pursuit of the Millennium*, Paladin Books 1970

Mircea Eliade, *Patterns in Comparative Religion*, Sheed and Ward 1971

T. H. Gaster, *The Scriptures of the Dead Sea Sect*, Secker and Warburg 1957

Michael Grant, *The Jews in the Roman World*, Weidenfeld and Nicholson 1973

E. Haenchen, *The Acts of the Apostles*, Blackwell 1971

R. P. C. Hanson, *Allegory and Event*, SCM Press 1959

Martin Hengel, *Judaism and Hellenism*, SCM Press 1974.

E. Hennecke, *New Testament Apocrypha* (two vols.), SCM Press 1973, 1974

John M. Hull, *Hellenistic Magic and the Synoptic Tradition*, SCM Press 1974

William James, *The Varieties of Religious Experience*, Fontana Books 1971

Joachim Jeremias, *Jerusalem in the Time of Jesus*, SCM Press 1969

Ernst Käsemann, *New Testament Questions of Today*, SCM Press 1969

H. C. Kee, *Community of the New Age*, SCM Press 1977

G. S. Kirk, *Myth. Its Meaning and Functions in Ancient and Other Cultures*, Cambridge University Press 1970

W. G. Kümmel, *Introduction to the New Testament*, SCM Press ²1975

—, *The New Testament. The History of the Investigation of its Problems*, SCM Press 1973

Edmund Leach (ed.), *The Structural Study of Myth and Totemism*, Tavistock Publications 1967

Claude Levi-Strauss, *The Savage Mind*, Weidenfeld and Nicholson 1966

H. Richard Niebuhr, *Christ and Culture*, Faber 1952

R. H. Pfeiffer, *A History of New Testament Times*, A. & C. Black 1954

Jean Piaget, *Structuralism*, Routledge 1971

O. Plöger, *Theocracy and Eschatology*, Blackwell 1968

Gerhard von Rad, *Wisdom in Israel*, SCM Press 1972

H. S. Reimarus, *Fragments*, SCM Press 1971

John A. T. Robinson, *Redating the New Testament*, SCM Press 1976

Gerd Theissen, *Sociology of Early Palestinian Christianity* (British title *The First Followers of Jesus*), SCM Press 1978

Max Weber, *The Sociology of Religion*, Methuen 1965

Brian Wilson, *Magic and the Millennium*, Heinemann Educational 1973

Peter Worsley, *The Trumpet Shall Sound*, Paladin Books 1970

# INDEXES

## Author Index

# Subject Index

# Scripture Index